THE WORLD'S HELICOPTERS

THE WORLD'S
HELICOPTERS

JOAN BRADBROOKE

 FOLLETT PUBLISHING COMPANY / CHICAGO

© F. D. Bradbrooke 1972
First published 1972 in Great Britain by
The Bodley Head Ltd.
Follett edition published 1973

ISBN 695-80377-8

Library of Congress Catalog Card Number: 72-97086

CONTENTS

ACKNOWLEDGMENTS

I would like to thank the following for help in the preparation of this book: Patricia and John Stroud particularly; H. Penrose; G. Quick, R. Gellatly and R. Crayton of Westland Aircraft Limited; C. H. Gibbs-Smith; D. W. H. Godfrey of Lockheed California; the Royal Aeronautical Society; the Vertical Lift Council of the American Aerospace Industries Association; many airlines and commercial operators round the world; and my daughter, Donna, for her practical help, interest and encouragement. The photographs appearing in this book were kindly supplied by the Bell Aircraft Corporation (page 26); Birks-Thorne Ltd (18); The Boeing Company (50, 73); Bristol Aeroplane Company (28); Bristol-Siddeley Engines Ltd (100); British European Airways (56, 81, 108); The General Electric Company (67); Hughes Tool Company, Aircraft Division (35); Informations Aéronautiques (76); New York Airways (54); Okanagan Helicopters (78); AB Hans Osterman (8); The Port of New York Authority (64, 66); Sabena (58); Sikorsky Aircraft (45, 46, 91, 93, 96, 98); John Stroud (23, 61, 68); Sud-Aviation/Aérospatiale (70, 87); John W. R. Taylor; Westland Helicopters Ltd (48, 51).

INTRODUCTION

The development and progress of the aeroplane and what it has achieved in almost seventy years since the Wright brothers made the first heavier-than-air flights in 1903 is spectacular, but what the helicopter has done in less than half that time is even more exciting. It is one of the most versatile – and perhaps complex – machines devised by man. Man may orbit the earth, he has walked on the moon, but it is a helicopter that rescues him after his return to earth.

Today helicopters are operating in most countries, from the Arctic to Borneo, in temperatures ranging from −50° F to 120° F, and from sea level to the high altitudes in the South American Andes and over the Swiss Alps. From pictures and reports in newspapers, on radio and on television, there can be few people who have not seen helicopters either with military and naval forces, rescuing people, recovering American astronauts after their splashdown in the Pacific Ocean, or in films.

A frequent sight if you live in London is a bright red helicopter dropping down over the trees at Hyde Park Corner into the gardens of Buckingham Palace – on occasions piloted by HRH the Prince Philip Duke of Edinburgh – or, in Washington, a Presidential helicopter landing on the White House lawns. In Paris visiting dignitaries are now brought by helicopter from Orly Airport to Les Invalides, the Air France terminal building in the centre of the city, instead of by the much slower motorcade with outriders and consequent traffic jams.

Numerous people who are afraid of flying – and there are many still – accept flights in helicopters quite happily. Perhaps it is the nearness to the ground – often 1,000 or 3,000 ft only – and the lack of speed, particularly at take-off and landing compared with jetliners, which contribute to a greater feeling of safety, together with the intimate view of the countryside which gives a familiar world an entirely different aspect. Whether flying in one of the small two- to three-seat helicopters, some of which almost resemble a goldfish bowl, looking down from a height of a few hundred feet into the tops of trees, or from a helicopter airliner, there is a fascination about this type of flying unlike any other.

1

Rotary Wings

The prime necessity for any heavier-than-air flying machine is a lifting medium. The conventional aeroplane obtains its lift from its fixed wings which are dependent on the forward speed produced by the engine. Control sections – elevators, ailerons and rudders – enable the aeroplane to change direction and altitude, but its support and control in flight depend entirely on adequate forward speed.

The word helicopter is derived from the Greek helix (spiral) and pteron (wing). The helicopter obtains its lift from one or more power-driven horizontal rotors or blades with a fixed, substantially vertical shaft. In other words it has its wings on top and is often called a rotary-wing aircraft or rotorcraft. Varying the angular setting of these rotors enables the helicopter to perform its unique manoeuvres – to take-off and land vertically, to fly sideways or

backwards, or to remain stationary in the air – to hover. A small auxiliary rotor at the tail is used on most single-rotor helicopters to supply directional control and to prevent torque, that is, the tendency of the fuselage to turn in a direction opposite to the rotation of the main rotor, and this is known as the anti-torque rotor. Some helicopters overcome this problem of torque by having two main rotors rotating in opposite directions – contra-rotating.

A simple experiment to give some indication of the forces of lift which act on an aeroplane's wing and a helicopter's rotors is to put your arm out of the window of a moving car. The arm should be held horizontally straight with the palm of the hand facing down. Turn your hand upward a little and at once you will feel your arm being pulled up. This happens because your hand forces the air passing

◀ Winter scene in the Stockholm archipelago with an Ostermans Aero Bell 47 delivering the mail.

over it to travel a greater distance, and faster, to meet the air moving underneath. The air on top is 'stretched' and becomes thinner, or less dense, so it presses down on your hand with less force than the air underneath which is somewhat compressed or 'thicker', so that it develops increased pressure and pushes up, making your hand move upwards. Simply, this is known as aerodynamic lift and is the way the air acts on the wing of an aeroplane as it moves forward and on the rotors of the helicopter as they rotate. Before an aeroplane or a helicopter can fly, the force applied to the wing or the rotor must be greater than the weight of the whole machine.

Air pressure on opposite sides of a surface can be varied by changing the angle at which the surface meets the air; this is known as angle of attack. A piece of cardboard held up on a windy day is all the apparatus needed to illustrate this.

In a helicopter the angular setting of the rotor blades is known as pitch, and when an equal alteration of blade angle is made on all the blades of a rotor, in the same direction, it is known as collective pitch control. When the pitch of each blade is altered in turn it is known as cyclic pitch control.

In the pioneering years the helicopter, even more than the conventional aeroplane, suffered from the lack of a suitable light-weight engine, because a helicopter requires a powerplant of much greater output than a fixed-wing aeroplane. The very complexity of the helicopter and the problems of controlling it in flight inevitably meant that all the first successful aircraft had fixed wings.

2

The History of the Helicopter

Man's search for the conquest of the air goes back to Daedalus and Icarus in Greek mythology, Wayland the Smith in the Norse sagas and Bladud the Flying King of Great Britain in 850 BC. Ancient China is believed to have known something of the principles of vertical flight, but until recently Leonardo da Vinci, the Italian painter, sculptor, anatomist, mechanician and scientist, was credited with having made the first model around 1486–90 of what he called a helical screw. This was mounted on a vertical shaft and powered by a spring mechanism and of it da Vinci wrote: 'I find that if this instrument made with a screw be well made – that is to say, made of linen of which the pores are stopped up with starch – and be turned swiftly, the said screw will make its spiral in the air and it will rise high.' Da Vinci recorded his ideas, with sketches, but his papers were not published until the second half of the nineteenth century or his several ideas on flight might have had more impact.

About a dozen years ago a Frenchman noticed in the museum at Le Mans a painting of the Madonna and Child by an unknown artist, dating from about 1460, in which the Christ child is holding what appears to be a small toy helicopter. Even more recently, the well-known aeronautical historian Charles Gibbs-Smith, going through a work in which the author had collected numerous drawings which appeared in medieval illuminated manuscripts, found a number described as of 'windmill toys' – there can be few children who have not played with the little stick with two or four 'blades' or sails rotating freely on a nail driven into the stick, called by the French a moulinet à vent. But he also

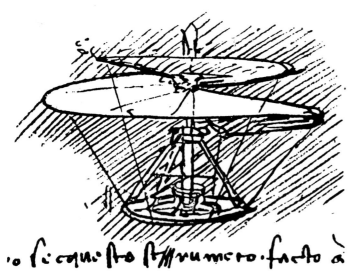

Leonardo da Vinci's drawing of his helical screw helicopter design, 1486–90.

found, dated circa 1325, an illustration of what he describes as 'a proper string-pull helicopter model of the same type as that in the Le Mans picture.' The original is in a Flemish illuminated manuscript in the Royal Library at Copenhagen.

Gibbs-Smith suggests that the inspiration for both the Le Mans and Copenhagen examples was the tower type of windmill common to Europe – whose origins are even now very obscure – and which first appeared in pictorial form about 1290, in the *Windmill Psalter* which is in the British Museum.

There is, however, some evidence to suggest that these illustrations were only portrayals of momentum toys, the chief of which is the yoyo which was even known to the ancient Greeks.

Da Vinci's idea of a helicopter screw, or the windmill toy, was revived by a French mathematician, Paucton, in 1768, in his 'Pterophore' as he called it. This was fitted with two screws, one to sustain the machine and the other to propel it. A few years later two other Frenchmen, Launoy and Bienvenu, gave the first practical demonstration of the principles of the helicopter and the airscrew. Their model consisted of twin two-bladed rotors which were wire frames covered with silk and which were contra-rotated by a bow-string mechanism. It was demonstrated before the Académie des Sciences in Paris in 1784 and flew successfully.

In 1796 (a date sometimes given as 1792, but now believed to be 1796) Sir George Cayley, known not only as the 'Father of British Aeronautics', but also recognised internationally as the true inventor of the aeroplane and the founder of the science of aeronautics, began his first experiments in heavier-than-air flight with an improved version of Launoy's and Bienvenu's little toy (one of which he had seen without knowing its origin). Cayley's version of the contra-rotating rotors were feathers stuck in corks and operated by a bowstring, which he did not

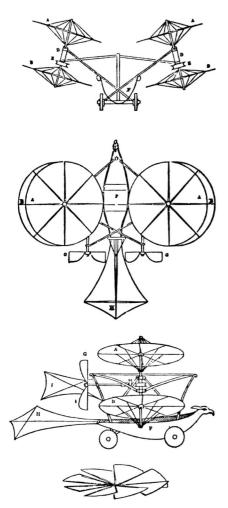

Sir George Cayley's design for a helicopter, 1843. The forward propulsion propellers are not shown in the front elevation.

publish until 1809 but which was widely copied. When he did publish he wrote: 'As it may be an amusement to some of your readers to see a machine rise in the air by mechanical means, I will conclude my present communication by describing an instrument of this kind, which anyone can construct at the expense of ten minutes' labour. A and B are two corks, into each of which are inserted four wing feathers, from any bird, so as to be slightly inclined like the sails of a windmill, but in opposite directions in each set. A round shaft is fixed in the A cork, which ends in a sharp point. At the upper part of the cork B is fixed a whalebone bow, having a small pivot hole in its centre to receive the point of the shaft. The bow is then to be strung equally on each side to the upper portion of the shaft, and the little machine is completed. Wind up the string by turning the flyers different ways, so that the spring of the bow may unwind them with their anterior edges ascending. Then place the cork with the bow attached to it upon a table, and with a finger on the upper cork press strongly enough to prevent the string from unwinding and, taking it away suddenly, the machine will rise to the ceiling.'

In 1853 Cayley returned to helicopters, having in the meantime published a number of important papers on aeronautics and made and flown both model and full-scale gliders, and – in 1843 – described an 'Aerial Carriage' which had contra-rotating rotors (rotors turning in opposite directions) on each side of a body which were to be used for taking off, and with two pusher propellers for horizontal flight. This was one of the first designs for what are now called convertiplanes – an aircraft which in vertical or hovering flight derives most of its lift from a power-driven rotor system and, in forward or horizontal flight, derives its lift from fixed wings.

Cayley's 1853 design for a helicopter, which was to be his last aeronautical work – he died in 1857 at the age of 84 – was a single three-bladed rotor made of tin, the shaft resting in a hollowed-out handle; a strong pull on a cord wound round the shaft rotated the rotor. The document describing this states: 'It will mount upwards of 90 ft into the air.' This document and drawings are preserved in the British Patent Office in London.

The first helicopter patent accepted by the British Patent Office, in 1859, was by another Englishman, Henry Bright, for a design for an aircraft with two contra-rotating co-axial two-blade rotors mounted on a single vertical shaft. This is a layout, modified, which has been adopted for a number of twentieth-century types of helicopters.

During the next fifty years many imaginative attempts and designs were made, and among the most noteworthy attempts during these years were the Vicomte de Ponton d'Amécourt's model with contra-rotating propellers worked by steam; the more successful models of another Frenchman, Alphonse Pénaud, in 1870; the work of the Russian Rykachev who began investigating aerial propellers in 1860, and in 1871 conducted experiments with a small four-blade rotor; Achenbach in Germany who, in 1874, had a design for an aircraft with a single rotor and a transverse airscrew to counteract torque; and the Italian Enrico Forlanini's steam-driven model, which had contra-rotating rotors like paddles and in 1877 climbed to a height of about forty feet, remaining airborne for twenty seconds.

Pénaud, but for his death at the age of thirty in 1880, might have contributed much to aeronautics because like Cayley all his work was scientific, but he has one link with modern times. In his first model helicopters in 1870 he replaced the whalebone or steel bow, used by Cayley and others as motive power, with strands of twisted India rubber. Not only did this work much better, but it is still used today by aero modellers.

Not until four years after the Wright brothers had achieved the first heavier-than-air controlled flights did the first full-size man-carrying helicopters appear, and both were French. In 1907 Louis Breguet and Professor Richet built a full-size four-rotor helicopter powered by a 45 hp Antoinette

The first man-carrying free flight by a helicopter was made by Paul Cornu's twin-rotor machine in November 1907.

engine. This machine lifted its pilot to a height of some two feet and later to five feet, but the machine had to be steadied by a man stationed at the end of each of the four arms supporting the rotors.

The first man-carrying free flight of a helicopter was made by another Frenchman, Paul Cornu, whose twin-rotor machine, powered by a 24 hp Antoinette engine, got off the ground although only to a height of about one foot for twenty seconds, in

November 1907, just a few weeks after the Breguet-Richet flight. Later Cornu's machine made take-offs to just over six feet but neither of these machines was successful and their development was abandoned. Little was heard of Cornu after this but Breguet built many famous aeroplanes and returned to helicopter design in the 1930s.

Ten years before these Frenchmen succeeded in precariously lifting themselves a few inches vertically into the air, an Englishman, B. R. Benen, had got as far as patenting a helicopter which would have a propeller for traction, and use an anti-torque tail rotor of which the blades could be angled at various settings to change the sideway pull for steering. The main lifting rotor blades also could be altered in angle as they rotated to increase or decrease the lift in expectation that this would give vertical control (Patent 9864). In 1905 E. R. Mumford patented a helicopter with tiltable rotors arranged in pairs of three each side of the main body, as well as a helicopter with paired overlapping and intermeshing rotors in order to give a more compact arrangement to his first idea. He and his partner, J. Pollock Brown, were experimental engineers at the great Scottish ship-building firm of William Denny & Brothers at Dumbarton, and had particular responsibility for the theory of ships' propellers. So strong a case did they present to the management for the helicopter that for some years from 1909 onwards they were allowed to experiment with a six-rotor full-sized machine to which they made many modifications in the next few years, but experiments had to stop with the outbreak of the 1914–18 war.

In 1912, J. C. Ellehammer, a Dane, built and demonstrated successfully a helicopter powered by a 36 hp engine, also of his own design. Earlier he had experimented with conventional aeroplanes and he is credited with having made the first flight in Denmark – in 1906. His helicopter had rotors and a conventional propeller, both driven by the same engine, and was what would now be classed as a compound helicopter. The rotors consisted of two contra-rotating rings each with six vanes at intervals around the perimeter. The angle of the rotor vanes could be altered in flight. This was one of the earliest examples of cyclic pitch control. Ellehammer continued to test this machine for three or four years until it was wrecked.

During the 1914–18 war the Austro-Hungarian army had a tethered helicopter designed and built by Theodore von Karman, who was to become one of the great figures in aeronautics, and Petroczy. Intended for use as an observation platform, it climbed to about 150 ft and could remain airborne for about an hour.

In the early 1920s short flights in helicopters of varying degrees of complexity were made in several parts of the world. Among the most noteworthy were the machines built by G. de Bothezat and Henry Berliner in the USA, Oehmichen in France, Pescara in Spain and France, and von Baumhauer in the Netherlands. The de Bothezat helicopter had four rotors, weighed 4,000 lb and in 1923 flew successfully with a pilot and three passengers. It was the first helicopter to be ordered by the US Army Air

Service. Henry Berliner, carrying on earlier work of his father's, built several helicopters, but the most successful was built around a Nieuport Scout aeroplane of the 1914–18 war. The Nieuport's wings were replaced by a pair of rotors, one on each side.

In 1923 in the United Kingdom the Air Ministry offered a prize of £50,000 for a successful helicopter which might well have been won by Louis Brennan, an elderly Irish-born inventor who had submitted a novel design for a helicopter to the British Government in 1919. It was accepted and work on it was begun, in secret, at the Royal Aircraft Establishment at Farnborough. The Brennan helicopter had a 60-ft diameter rotor driven by two propellers, at the tips of the blades, themselves powered by a 230 hp rotary air-cooled engine which was mounted centrally. A number of tethered flights with this helicopter were made at Farnborough but unfortunately it crashed in 1925. Because there was much scepticism of helicopters in the country, even among the learned societies, probably because of the promise shown by the Autogiro, the Government abandoned the project.

In France, Oehmichen, a young engineer connected with the Peugeot works, built a helicopter which had four rotors and eight propellers, all driven by one engine – a 120 hp Le Rhône rotary, later replaced by a 180 hp Gnome. Five of the propellers turning in a horizontal plane were for lateral control, two acted as pusher propellers for forward propulsion, and the remaining one, mounted at the nose, was for steering the helicopter. Numerous successful flights were made with this machine and on 4 May 1924 it completed the first officially observed flight by a helicopter over a closed-circuit course of 1 km.

Raoul Pescara built several helicopters during the years 1919–26, at first in Spain and later in France. His third machine had two contra-rotating co-axial rotors each with four pairs of blades driven through a clutch and gearing by a 180 hp Hispano Suiza engine. With this helicopter Pescara achieved horizontal flights of up to 800 yards and up to ten minutes duration. His work is important because of the control system he used. Horizontal flight was obtained by sloping a control column in the required direction, which changed the pitch of all the rotor blades during the cycle of rotation. The incidence of all the blades could also be altered so that their pitch changed by the same amount simultaneously to increase or decrease lift. The principles in these controls are applied in modern helicopters and are known as cyclic pitch control and collective pitch control. His method also enabled the rotors to act as windmills to provide some lift in case of engine failure. He seems to have been one of the first to recognise the importance of this but, in spite of these innovations,

Pescara's helicopters were not successful and he abandoned serious work on them, returning to Spain in 1925.

The first helicopter to look anything like the one we know today was that of von Baumhauer in the Netherlands. He built and flew, in 1925, the first single-rotor helicopter which also had one of the first tail rotors to counteract torque, or the turning moment, but the main and tail rotors were driven by separate engines. The machine was badly damaged before extensive tests could be made. Hitherto all helicopter designs had had at least two main rotors and looked clumsy, complicated contraptions as, indeed, they were. Von Baumhauer's design of a single main rotor and small tail rotor is the basic configuration of many helicopters today and was far in advance of its time, although the Russian Yuriev is said to have conceived an anti-torque layout in 1909.

The first really successful rotating-wing aircraft which was to contribute much to the successful evolution of the helicopter was the gyroplane invented and first flown in Spain by Juan de la Cierva in 1923 and which he called the 'Autogiro'. This became a registered name reserved for Cierva types, but it has been loosely applied throughout the world to any type of gyroplane. Strictly, the word, if used, should be spelt autogyro.

A gyroplane is a rotorcraft which derives substantially all its lift from a freely-rotating rotor system and its forward motion from an engine and propeller. This is the essential difference between the gyroplane and the helicopter; the rotors are *not* power-driven. Also the airflow is up through the rotor, whereas in the helicopter it is down through the rotor.

Cierva's Autogiro consisted of a conventional aeroplane fuselage and tail unit with an engine driving a normal propeller in the nose; in the earlier models four blades, but in later types, three blades, resembling long, narrow and flexible wings, were attached to a nearly vertical shaft which was inclined slightly backwards. These 'wings' behaved like a windmill, being kept in rotation and generating lift by the forward motion of the whole aeroplane. The Autogiro could take off in a much shorter distance than conventional aeroplanes, and land with a short run of a few yards only, but it was not capable of hovering flight.

Cierva had begun by designing fixed-wing aircraft and explained later that he turned to the Autogiro in 1918 after seeing an aeroplane crash because of loss of speed near the ground; he wanted to develop a safer aeroplane which would not be dependent completely on the application of mechanical power. His first attempts were unsuccessful but in his 1923

◄ Louis Brennan's helicopter at Farnborough in the early 1920s.
The designer is standing in front of the machine.

machine he employed an entirely new principle of rotor design which not only solved his own immediate problems but was to lead eventually to the first controllable and successful helicopters.

Instead of attaching the rotors rigidly to the shaft, Cierva provided a hinge at the root of each blade which allowed the blades to flap freely up and down while rotating. One of the difficulties in the control of helicopters had been the unequal lift between the retreating and advancing rotor blades. Cierva's articulated hinges enabled each retreating blade to flex downward as the advancing blade's air speed lifted it up, so that the lift forces were in balance.

Through the instigation of a British firm, G. & J. Weir Limited, which was to do much on the engineering side to advance the Autogiro, Cierva came to England in 1925 to demonstrate his Autogiro and remained, forming his own company the following year. For the next ten years he designed many types of Autogiro of which perhaps the best-known were the C.19, in which for the first time he introduced automatic starting of the rotor which hitherto had been started by pulling on a rope wound round the shaft; and the C.30, in which the engine was used directly to drive the rotor blades for take-off, was then de-clutched and drove only the propeller. The C.30 also had a new control system which enabled the rotor head to be tilted in any direction. Last of

the Cierva Autogiros was the C.40 which incorporated a direct drive to the rotor; this was used only on the ground to drive the rotor initially to achieve a jump take-off to a height of some twenty feet before forward flight began.

Cierva Autogiros were sold to many countries throughout the world and were built under licence in Great Britain, France, Germany, Italy, Japan and the USA. They were used in many rôles including operations from ships, by police forces for traffic control and, in the USA, for an experimental mail service from the roof of the Philadelphia Post Office. During the 1939–45 war they were used in Great Britain for radar trials and for communications work.

Juan de la Cierva was killed in an airliner crash in December 1936. With his death and the successful evolution of the helicopter soon afterwards, active development of the gyroplane virtually ceased, although during the past fifteen years interest has revived, especially for small single- or two-seat types for private or sporting flying and special duties. By the end of 1969 eleven firms were building gyroplanes, four in the United Kingdom, and one each in Canada, Czechoslovakia, Denmark, Finland, Germany, South Africa and the USA.

Cierva's influence was seen in several helicopters of the 1930s. In Italy, d'Ascanio produced a co-axial machine with two 40-ft diameter rotors free to flap about horizontal hinges which could also rotate about ball bearings for changes in pitch. In 1930 this machine set up the first Fédération Aéronautique Internationale (FAI) distance, height and endurance records in the helicopter class, which included a duration flight of some nine minutes, a closed-circuit flight over a one-km course and a vertical ascent to twenty feet, hovering there for one and a half minutes. This performance was not very impressive when compared with Cierva's flight from Croydon to Le Bourget (Paris) on 18 September 1928 in his C.8L Autogiro, the first crossing of the English Channel by a rotary-wing aircraft.

Nevertheless, progress was being made and in 1935 Louis Breguet re-entered the helicopter field with the Breguet-Dorand 'Gyroplane Laboratoire', a co-axial type with hinged contra-rotating two-blade metal rotors of large diameter, and powered by a 350 hp Hispano Suiza 90 engine. Between December 1935 and November 1936 this machine set up new helicopter records of all kinds. It had good control and stability and did much useful experimental work before it was destroyed in an accident.

Performance of the Breguet-Dorand helicopter, however, was completely overshadowed by the German Focke-Achgelis Fw 61 which, in 1937 and 1938, not only broke all existing international records but established new standards with a speed of 76 mph, altitude of 8,000 ft, duration of one hour and twenty minutes, and distance in a straight line of 143 miles. The Fw 61 had two rotors mounted on steel-tube outriggers, or lateral booms, extending from the fuselage. The fully-articulated three blades of the rotors could have the blade angle increased or decreased to provide lateral movement of the machine.

The manoeuvrability and controllability of the Fw 61 was dramatically demonstrated inside the 250 ft by 100 ft Deutschland Halle sports stadium in Berlin in February 1938 by Germany's famous woman test pilot Hanna Reitsch. The Fw 61 also made the first helicopter flights between cities – from Bremen to Berlin. A later development, the Fa 223, was used by the Germans during the last two years of the 1939–45 war to carry supplies to troops in mountainous regions. Another successful German designer at this time was Anton Flettner and although his work is not generally as well known as the Focke designs, several Flettner types were used by the German Navy for shipboard reconnaissance duties in the Baltic and Mediterranean from 1942.

The man who finally developed the helicopter into a fully practicable and controllable aircraft, capable of being produced in quantity, able to carry a payload and do a useful job of work, is usually acknowledged to be Igor Ivanovitch Sikorsky. Born in Kiev

Father of the modern helicopter. Igor Sikorsky flying his VS-300,
seen here in modified form.

in 1889, he designed and built a helicopter in 1909 and another in 1910. Both were unsuccessful and he turned to fixed-wing aircraft, designing and building among other types the first multi-engined aircraft in 1912. Leaving Russia during the Revolution, Sikorsky went first to France and then, in 1919, to the USA. In 1923, with the help of friends, he founded his own company and designed and built a series of some of the most successful flying-boats of the day, which pioneered the first commercial airline services from the USA to Hongkong in 1937, and made one of the first commercial survey flights across the North Atlantic.

Over the years Sikorsky had from time to time taken out an occasional patent on some phase of helicopter design, and made notes and sketches of possible projects, and had obviously kept in touch with developments in Europe. Thirty years after building his first helicopter, he flew his third design – the VS-300 – on 14 September 1939. During its initial flights the VS-300 was tethered to the ground, then on 13 May 1940 the first free flight was made, and on 6 May 1941, with Sikorsky at the controls, the VS-300 established a world helicopter endurance record – previously held by the Fw 61 – by remaining in the air for 1 hr 32 min 26·1 sec.

For three years Sikorsky made continuous tests with the VS-300, trying many configurations; it is

The Sikorsky R-4 was the first production helicopter. A Royal Air Force example, the Hoverfly, is seen flying at Farnborough.

said that he made at least eighteen major modifications to this experimental helicopter. It began with a 75 hp Lycoming four-cylinder engine and finished with a 150 hp Franklin engine, and finally had a fabric-covered fuselage, tricycle undercarriage and open seat for the pilot in the front. Its single main rotor, with anti-torque tail rotor, was a configuration Sikorsky helicopters have retained ever since.

Three early Sikorsky helicopters. *Left to right:* R-4, R-5 and R-6.

In 1943, by which time development of the first production Sikorsky helicopter – the R-4 series – was well advanced, the historic VS-300 was flown to the Henry Ford Museum at Dearborn, Michigan, where it has remained.

Once the success of the helicopter had been established by Sikorsky, other American types emerged and soon after the 1939–45 war several countries in Europe produced a number of interesting and successful helicopters.

3

The Development of the Helicopter

A much-quoted statement by Lee S. Johnson, as president of the Sikorsky Division of the United Aircraft Corporation some twenty years after the first successful Sikorsky helicopter was achieved, is: 'Before Igor Sikorsky flew the VS-300 there was no helicopter industry; after he flew it there was.' Certainly by the end of the 1940s at least four other companies in the USA were building helicopters of their own design, as were companies in the United Kingdom and in France. Today, apart from the USA and the USSR, the major countries building helicopters are the United Kingdom, France, West Germany, Italy and Japan.

Recently the US military forces were training more helicopter pilots than fixed-wing pilots and helicopters comprised some 35 per cent of the USA's military manned fleets.

Soon after the 1939–45 war the first civil types were produced, the American Bell Model 47 being the first helicopter in the world to receive a type approval certificate, in 1946, for commercial use; variants of this model have been built ever since. In that same year the first Sikorsky commercial type, the S-51, made its first flight, but in spite of the fact that in the past thirty years the speed of the helicopter has increased fourfold and its gross weight is 100 times greater, progress has been slow in many respects.

The basic disadvantages of the helicopter have always been its mechanical complexity, high initial first cost, high maintenance costs, vibration, noise, instability and difficult flying qualities in certain weather conditions. Another problem is its inefficient range for the payload it can carry and its lack of speed. Economically the pure helicopter is unlikely

The Bell 47 was the first helicopter to receive civil certification. A Helicopter Air Service Bell 47 flying on US Air Mail Route 96 is seen arriving at a Chicago suburban heliport. The wind direction indicator is beyond the fence to the left of the gate.

ever to compare with fixed-wing aircraft. Nevertheless, over the years a great deal has been done to improve its handling qualities and other handicaps, although mechanically it is more complex than ever. A good idea of the progress made during the past 25 years can be gained from Chapter 11.

The development of vibration absorbers has helped that problem; electronic devices such as the automatic pilot and automatic stabilising equipment now make it possible to fly a stable flight path whatever the helicopter's speed. These units together with others for navigation have simplified instrument flying in most weather conditions.

Noise is still a problem but is not confined to helicopters, and some commercial types are now comparable with certain fixed-wing types. In most built-up areas the public is not used to helicopters so their noise makes a substantial impact, one of the reasons probably for the lack of city-centre heliports. Yet it is doubtful whether the noise a helicopter makes is much more objectionable than, say, a heavy truck or a powerful motor-cycle. Designers everywhere are trying to produce quieter engines; recently the US Navy has been trying out on an S-51 mufflers for intakes and exhausts but such modifications add additional weight, complication and expense.

One of the drawbacks of the helicopter is its lack of speed. On all rotary-wing aircraft there is a forward speed at which drag (the aerodynamic force caused by the resistance of the atmosphere to the forward motion of a body), vibration and loss of lift limit further improvement, especially with hinged rotors. The retreating blades have a tendency to stall, that is when the angle of attack (the angle of the wing, or rotor, and the air which strikes it) becomes so great that the air flow over the top of the blade breaks down and becomes turbulent; at the same time the advancing blades reach a high forward speed and become subject to the effects of the compressibility of air, which become marked as the speed of sound is approached at the tips of the rotors. A practical limit for forward speed of the pure helicopter at present is little more than 200–250 mph. The efficiency of the rotor cannot compare with a fixed-wing aircraft in forward flight. This is why stub-wings have been added to some helicopters to give more lift, or a propeller, which makes it a 'compound' helicopter; it has also led to the development of the 'convertiplane' which uses rotors for take-off and landing and wings and propellers for forward flight.

Over the years it is doubtful whether any type of aircraft, except the Anglo-French Concorde super-sonic transport, has been subjected to quite so much testing as the helicopter, and many special ground testing rigs have been devised for rotors and for hovering flight. In fact, the rotor test tower established by the Bristol Aeroplane Company at Filton, Bristol, just after the 1939–45 war to test the Bristol 171 Sycamore was the first of its kind in the world.

The complicated mechanisms of the helicopter make rigorous testing essential and apart from research into vibration, new designs of blades, rotor heads, transmissions, gear boxes – which may them-selves be subjected to a thousand hours and more of testing – new materials and so on, every part and every system is stringently proven. Anything up to ten years is now accepted as the time limit for any new aircraft from drawing board to first flight and the helicopter is no exception, but of this time eighteen months to two years or more may be spent on ground tests and tethered flight before a new helicopter goes into production. When it does, frequently it incorporates well-tried components from earlier types. For instance, the very big Soviet Mi-12 is understood to use the same rotors as the Mi-10.

Like all aircraft, helicopters are designed for a specific purpose which determines their specifications and their performance characteristics. They may be single-seat types or carry up to 250 people; they may lift loads of 80,000 lb or more; and their rotor diameters may be anything from 25 ft to 114 ft.

The single-rotor helicopter is still the most common layout and may have from two to six blades; these may be of metal, wood or a composite material. The undercarriage may comprise wheels, sometimes retractable, skids or floats; some helicopters have a flying-boat type of hull and some, in addition to wheels, have inflatable flotation gear for use in emergency alightings on water.

There may be one, two, three or four engines, either

The Bristol 173 was a twin-engined helicopter with tandem contra-rotating rotors.

piston (known as reciprocating engines) or gas-turbines. These latter are usually turboshaft engines, that is gas-turbines designed to drive a power shaft through a reduction gear rather on the lines of the propeller-turbines for fixed-wing aircraft. The gas-turbine may also be what is called a 'free' turbine if it is not mechanically connected to the compressor and rotor; in this case the gases from the first turbine pass into a second, co-axial free turbine which drives the rotor.

Piston engines used today may be anything from 160 hp to 1,700 hp and gas-turbines range from 260 shp to 6,500 shp. The engines may be located behind the pilot or cockpit, occasionally in the nose of the fuselage, but most frequently on top of the fuselage, on each side of it or on booms extending from the fuselage. With three engines the third is usually aft of the main rotor shaft. Ram jets (engines which only work at high forward speed as air is rammed into them) have been used and tip jets – that is propulsion units mounted on the blade tips.

The application of the gas-turbine in the early 1950s, and the development of the small gas-turbine particularly, probably did more for the advancement of the helicopter than anything. It has a better power-to-weight ratio than the piston engine, weighs less and can be smaller, so taking up less space inside the helicopter and leaving more room for payload, and it is cheaper to operate and maintain. Although the initial cost of the turbine is greater than that of the piston engine, the higher cost is offset by improved performance, permitting operations at higher altitudes, and by increased reliability.

The following are the main types of rotor used today:

Single rotor with anti-torque tail rotor.

Tandem rotor, one rotor forward and one aft, which may or may not be intermeshing; both rotors are driven synchronously from a main power supply. This type of helicopter was first perfected by an American, F. N. Piasecki, in 1945, whose company became the Vertol Aircraft Corporation and since 1960 has been the Vertol Division of the Boeing Company. The CH-47A Chinook is the best-known example of this type of helicopter.

Side-by-side configuration. This also may be either intermeshing or non-intermeshing. Like the tandem rotor the twin rotor eliminates the need for an anti-torque tail rotor. Known as 'synchropter' rotors, the twin rotors are carried on angular masts on each side of the fuselage. The American Kaman company adopted this configuration for some of its earlier models.

Co-axial contra-rotating rotors. The Russian Kamov types use this configuration.

Rotor heads also vary and the basic configurations today are:

The articulate (or hinged) rotor with separate and lagging hinges so that the individual blades are free to flap, drag and change pitch. This type is basically unchanged from Cierva's design.

The teetering rotor, usually used on small helicopters with two-bladed rotors, which incorporates a single flapping (teetering) hinge.

The semi-rigid rotor in which the blades do not flap individually but can flap like a see-saw about a central gimbal. The Anglo-French SA-341 Gazelle is an example.

The rigid (or hingeless) rotor in which the blades are cantilevered from the hub with freedom to rotate only about the feathering axis. This rigid rotor was first perfected by the Lockheed Aircraft Corporation in the USA in 1959, in the experimental CL-475, and demonstrated a number of advantages. It had a high degree of

inherent stability and of control power, a much greater centre-of-gravity range than the hinged-rotor helicopter and low vibration levels. It also indicated the possibility of increased speeds. In addition the rigid rotor improves the handling qualities of the helicopter, and removing the hinges and their complicated mechanisms simplifies production and maintenance. The Lockheed AH-56A Cheyenne and the German Bölkow Bö 105 have rigid rotors.

Helicopters are usually classified as ultra-light, as in two/three-seat trainers and utility craft; light, as in five/six-seat general purpose (utility, executive) craft; medium, that is ten/twelve-seat transports, general purpose; heavy, twenty-six/thirty-three-seat transports and cargo craft; lift cranes: and combat helicopters, fitted with armament of various kinds for anti-tank or escort duties.

The development of the helicopter has lagged far behind that of the fixed-wing aircraft but rotary-wing aircraft have come a long way in thirty years.

Juan de la Cierva made the first crossing of the English Channel by a rotary-wing aircraft in his Autogiro in 1928; almost forty years later, on 1 June 1967, two Sikorsky S-61 military helicopters made the first nonstop helicopter crossing of the North Atlantic from New York to Le Bourget. They were refuelled in flight nine times on their 4,270 mile journey. A helicopter flight has also been made between the United Kingdom and Australia. This journey of 11,184 miles flown in $97\frac{1}{2}$ hours is believed to be the longest flight ever made by a helicopter. The actual helicopter was a Westland Wessex 60 and, of course, it made many intermediate landings.

At the present time new materials are being developed, metals which in some cases are stronger than steel and yet lighter than aluminium, and composites of plastics and various new carbon fibres, which will find their uses in engines and structures, whilst improvements in electronics will enable greater accuracy and reliability in guidance and navigation. All these could speed the development of the helicopter in the coming years.

◀ The Kaman HOK-1 had side-by-side intermeshing rotors. This Kaman is seen with 'Bear Paw' undercarriage for use on snow, mud or sand.

	Rotor diameter		Length		Passengers	Loaded weight	Cruising speed	Range
USA								
Bell 47B	35′	1½″	27′	4″*	1–2	2,078 lb	92 mph	214 miles
Sikorsky S-51	48′	0″	44′	11½″*	3	4,900 lb	80 mph	260 miles
UNITED KINGDOM								
Bristol 171	48′	6½″	46′	8″⊖	2–3	5,200 lb	132 mph	230 miles

* Length of fuselage excluding rotors
⊖ Minimum length

4

Flying a Helicopter

The modern helicopter, particularly those used by the naval and military services and by commercial operators, is a complex machine with many instruments especially designed and adapted for flight in most conditions. The cockpit in fact can look like that of a conventional airliner. Helicopters for training and private operation have fewer instruments, and the cockpit has the same basic flight instruments as a fixed-wing aircraft such as air-speed indicator, altimeter, compass, fuel, oil and temperature gauges, radio and engine rpm gauge or tachometer. For the helicopter the tachometer is in fact two instruments with one clock face and an inner and outer scale. In those of British make a long needle indicates the rotor rpm on the outer scale and a short needle the engine rpm on the inner scale; in US-made instruments these positions are reversed.

The two needles are superimposed when the clutch between engine and transmission is fully engaged and again in normal flight conditions.

The single-rotor helicopter with a two/four-blade main rotor and small anti-torque rotor at the tail being still the most common type in use is the one used in the following brief description of, basically, how a helicopter flies.

The rotor blades radiate symmetrically from a central hub, or head, on top of the fuselage; they are driven by an engine through a gear box and from this gear box also extends the drive shaft through the fuselage and boom extension housing to the gear box for the anti-torque tail rotor.

The pilot has four main controls:

The cyclic-pitch lever or stick, or control column as it is sometimes called, usually positioned between his knees.

The collective-pitch lever, which slants up at an angle on the left-hand side of the pilot's seat.

Rudder pedals and a *throttle control*. This latter is a motor-cycle type twist-grip throttle control mounted on the end of the collective-pitch lever. It controls the engine rpm to regulate the speed of the main rotor. Twisting the throttle outboard increases speed and twisting it inboard decreases speed.

All these controls are in constant and inter-related use.

Raising the collective-pitch lever increases the pitch of all the main rotor blades simultaneously, so that the resultant lift is vertical; lowering the lever makes the helicopter descend. Piston-engined helicopters are usually used for training, and normally they have a throttle cam mechanism in the collective-pitch system which automatically opens the engine throttle when the lever is raised to provide power for the climb, but the twist-grip throttle is needed for changes of flight condition to maintain constant rpm. Turboshaft-driven rotors and helicopters with gas-turbine engines have an automatic system of rotor rpm in powered flight.

For forward horizontal flight the cyclic-pitch stick is used. This changes the pitch of each rotor blade and tilts the rotor in the desired direction.

Tilting the rotor changes its lift from purely vertical to a combination of vertical and horizontal lift and thrust.

The rudder pedals operate the anti-torque rotor to balance torque and to turn the helicopter and work in the same way as the rudder controls of a fixed-wing aeroplane. By applying the left rudder the pitch of the anti-torque rotor is increased for a turn to the left and by applying the right pedal it is decreased for a turn to the right.

It is the co-ordination of these four controls which a student pilot may find difficult at first. In the conventional fixed-wing aeroplane there is an immediate change in the attitude of the aeroplane in response to control movement, but in a conventional hinged-rotor helicopter there is a time lag; with movement of the cyclic control stick for forward flight the rotor tilts first and then the fuselage. When the cyclic-pitch stick is moved from the hovering position there must be a movement of the collective-pitch lever to maintain height; at the same time this produces an increase of power which in turn causes an increase of main rotor torque which means using the pedals to increase tail rotor pitch and, simultaneously, the twist-grip throttle must be used to increase main rotor speed. The change from hovering flight to forward flight is known as translational flight.

As has been said, most gas-turbine powered heli-

A group of Hughes TH-55A training helicopters for the US Army ▶
seen awaiting delivery at Culver City, California.

copters now have automatic rpm control which makes the pilot's task easier, and with a rigid-rotor helicopter movement of the cyclic control stick gives almost simultaneous response of rotor and fuselage together.

To someone watching, hovering flight may look easy, but to maintain steady hovering the pilot will need to make constant small corrections with all controls – the cyclic-pitch stick to maintain position, collective-pitch lever to maintain height, rudder pedals to keep the heading direction, and the throttle to correct any change of rpm. It is this control co-ordination and learning to sense the need for control movement that takes time to learn. Someone once put it graphically, 'Skilled helicopter pilots fly as good horsemen ride, as part of the mount.'

It sounds complicated and in some senses it is, and there is much more to flying and understanding a helicopter than this brief account.

The question is often asked, 'Is it more difficult to fly a helicopter than a fixed-wing aircraft?' At first it is. Anyone who holds a Private Pilot's Licence for fixed-wing aircraft in the United Kingdom usually requires some five hours less flying instruction than an *ab-initio* helicopter trainee, who now has to have a minimum of thirty-five hours flying training and about forty hours ground training which includes such subjects as the theory of rotary-wing flight,

navigation, radio aids and instruments and air regulations. An *ab-initio* trainee is usually ready for his first solo flight after eight to ten hours flying instruction but must complete thirty-five hours in the air and pass both a flight test and a written examination before achieving a Private Pilot's Licence (Helicopter) – PPL (H). Before going solo he is also taught autorotation, a safety feature of the helicopter which goes back to Cierva's Autogiro. This is the ability of the rotor to autorotate in case of engine failure (a rare occasion nowadays) or if the pilot wishes to descend faster than he could do with power applied to the rotor. The definition of auto-rotation has been given as 'the process of producing lift with freely-rotating aerofoils by means of aero-dynamic forces resulting from an upward flow of air'. In powered flight the air flows into the rotor from above; in autorotation, or 'windmilling' as it is sometimes called, the engine is disengaged and the air flows into the rotor from underneath as the helicopter descends. The rotor still produces lift, with the blades at a low pitch angle, and all controls function normally.

Learning to fly a helicopter is expensive, £25–£35 an hour compared with some £6–£8 an hour on a fixed-wing aircraft, the cost in both cases depending on the type of aircraft. Light two-seat helicopters such as the Hughes 300 or Brantly B-2 are cheaper than Bells and Hillers, all of them American types. For the turbine-powered five-seat types flying costs may go to around £70 an hour. A PPL (H) is type-rated, that is to fly a different type of helicopter a pilot would have to satisfy an instructor after five hours flying as pilot-in-command of the new type as well as pass an oral examination on that type.

The main reason for the difference in cost of learning to fly a helicopter and a fixed-wing aircraft is the initial first cost of the helicopter and its operating and maintenance costs. For example, a new fixed-wing two/four-seat single-engined aeroplane, such as the Piper Cherokee 140B with a 150 hp engine, costs about £6,000–£8,000 depending on the equipment installed, whereas a Hughes 300 three-seat helicopter with a 180 hp engine, which is widely used in the USA for training, would cost more than £25,000.

Minimum requirements for a commercial pilot's licence are at least 150 hours flying time and some 400 hours other training.

The number of people who can fly helicopters is increasing all the time. Although most helicopter pilots are men, in the United Kingdom there are some half-dozen women licensed to fly them, of whom one is Sheila Scott who holds more fixed-wing light aviation records than anyone else. There is also one woman in the United Kingdom with a commercial helicopter licence. Some of the FAI helicopter records set up by the Soviet Union have been by women pilots.

Although a vehicle demanding pilot skill, the ability of the helicopter to fly sideways, backwards, forwards, to hover and to land and take off from such small spaces, makes it one of the most fascinating forms of flying.

5

The Helicopter in Military Service

Mobility has always been one of the most important factors for an army. In early wars horses and mules were used for moving supplies and artillery; motor transport, armoured fighting vehicles and tanks were introduced in the 1914–18 war, and in the 1939–45 war transport aircraft were used to carry airborne forces and for the dropping of parachutes with troops and supplies. These airborne operations lacked landing grounds, and parachute troops and supplies could be dispersed and scattered over quite a wide area, or shot down as sitting targets on their descent.

Although more than 400 Sikorsky R-4 helicopters and variants of the series – the first helicopters to go into large-scale production – were used during the last two years of the 1939–45 war by British and American forces from Burma to Alaska, mainly for

utility and rescue work, it was not until the Korean war (1950–53) that the flexibility of the helicopter was appreciated and its real military career started. By that time the helicopter had advanced in carrying capacity and performance and more types were available, but there were still problems, including the difficulties of operating at high altitudes and in hot countries where engine performance rapidly deteriorates.

During the Korean war helicopters were again used mainly for communications, observation and reconnaissance, transport of food and ammunition to otherwise inaccessible areas, rescue work and as aerial ambulances. More than 23,000 United Nations personnel were rescued from battlefield areas and flown to medical stations in the rear. Many pilots who had been shot down were also rescued. Both US

◀ The large twin-engined tandem-rotor Boeing-Vertol CH-47 Chinook is widely used by US forces. This one is ferrying a Bell Iroquois to a repair-ship off Vietnam.

Boeing-Vertol CH-46 twin-engined helicopters in the troop-carrying rôle. Troops disembark from the nearest aircraft while another flies off after unloading.

and Royal Navy aircraft carriers were used on commando-type operations, flying in marines by helicopters.

In the 1950s and early 1960s British forces used both British-designed helicopters such as the Bristol Sycamore and Belvedere, and Sikorsky types built under licence by Westlands (the S-51 Dragonfly, S-55 Whirlwind and S-58 Wessex) as well as the

Westland Scout and Wasp, on anti-terrorist operations and in trouble spots such as Malaya, Singapore, Cyprus, Aden and Borneo. Their duties were mainly reconnaissance, communications, supply and rescue, but the Belvedere could carry up to eighteen fully-equipped troops and the Wessex sixteen. During these operations there were many recoveries, especially in the Far East, of crippled fixed-wing aircraft which, but for the helicopters, would have had to be written off; the helicopters recovered them and flew them back to base, often over appallingly difficult country, to be repaired and flown again. This has been done extensively by the USA in Vietnam.

The French forces in Algeria and in Indo-China, a decade ago, used large numbers of Sud-Aviation and American-built helicopters for transporting troops and supplies and for commando-type operations. In Algeria, where much of the terrain is mountainous and ground troops would have taken days to cross or climb distances as short as ten miles, helicopters could drop them where they were required. Many valuable lessons about helicopters for military activities were learned during these 'counter-insurgency' or 'limited war' operations as they are called sometimes. One was that special training was needed even by experienced pilots for combat operations over hostile and difficult country, such as Algeria, where wide temperature variations exist and sudden high winds will tax the skill of even the most competent pilots.

Another was that the pilot and troop commander must be able to communicate with one another and that the pilot must be in overall command of the troops for any landing. There were a few occasions when the Army commander gave the order to disembark but the pilot, because of heavy enemy ground fire, decided to take-off again. Now, more often than not troops in forward areas disembark while the helicopter hovers a few feet above the ground.

Experiments with the arming of helicopters began in the 1950s. At first troops firing their rifles and sub-machine-guns from the open doors and the co-pilot firing from his window provided limited defensive cover; later, experimental armament systems were developed combining machine-guns, cannon and rockets fitted on each side of the nose, together with machine-guns mounted in the cabin doors. These systems could be installed or removed quickly. This is an important consideration for some countries with limited resources because it means that the helicopter can serve in a dual rôle, either defensive/offensive or for rescue or transport work.

Fixed forward-firing machine-guns proved not entirely satisfactory and even empty cartridge cases created problems, there being many instances of tail rotors being damaged by them, and therefore collector boxes for the empties had to be included on the mountings.

Adding armament added weight to the helicopter, but by the early 1960s gas-turbines had increased the reliability, power and performance of the helicopter, especially for operations in varying temperature conditions and at altitude.

The war in Vietnam has produced armament systems developed specifically for helicopters in both the defensive and offensive rôles. All services of the US armed forces, Air Force, Army, Navy and Marine are employed in this 'limited war', and it has often been called a helicopter war because with them a new concept of 'airmobility' was introduced by the US Army. From the beginning helicopters were used extensively, about a hundred helicopters being included in a number of US infantry divisions to replace trucks for moving men and supplies and for evacuating casualties. Ninety per cent of all US wounded are said to have been evacuated from Vietnam combat areas by helicopter, compared with about fifteen per cent during the Korean conflict.

For the US and South Vietnamese infantryman, helicopters carry him into battle, provide much of his fire support, most of his ammunition, food and equipment, and evacuate him if he is wounded.

In 1965, after some years of evaluation, tests and combat exercises against other Army and Air Force units in the USA, the First Air Cavalry Division of the US Army – the first unit of its kind in the world – arrived in South Vietnam. The Division had 400/450 helicopters and some 20,000 men, about one quarter of them mechanics. Backbone of the Air Cavalry equipment has been the Hughes OH-6A light observation helicopter (LOH), variants of the Bell UH-1B Iroquois, more commonly known as the Huey because it was originally designated by the Army HU-1 and so was soon nicknamed Huey by its crews. It is used for troop-carrying, aerial ambulance work, patrol and armed escort duties. Other standbys are the Boeing-Vertol Chinook, Bell Cobra (or Hueycobra) and the Sikorsky Skycrane.

In a typical airborne assault operation, after reconnaissance and observation by the LOH and other helicopters, troops are flown in by Hueys, the Chinooks bringing in guns, ammunition, rocket launchers and other supplies, which are usually slung from hooks underneath for faster unloading. The Chinooks can carry 24,000 lb of cargo internally or 20,000 lb externally, or 33/44 combat troops or 24 casualty stretcher patients. The Sikorsky Skycranes bring in the big howitzers and other bulky equipment. They can also be fitted with special containers,

known in Vietnam as Purple People Pods, which fit into the empty space behind the cabin. These containers can carry 45 fully-equipped combat troops or may be fitted out as field hospitals.

Once an operation has been completed, the armed helicopters having kept watch all the time, troops and guns are lifted to the next position or returned to base. Every helicopter flying in additional troops or supplies brings out casualties. As has been said, from lessons learned in the Algerian war, troops usually disembark while the helicopter hovers a few feet above the ground. Where the area is unsuitable for landing or hovering and only a few troops may be needed, they descend by ropes from the helicopter. In American parlance this is known as rapelling but in the Royal Air Force it is called to abseil. When a large-scale landing is required and the terrain is unsuitable even for helicopters, a landing strip must be built in the jungle or forest, and to achieve this engineers are lowered from the helicopter by special 250-ft rope ladders, something on the lines of the 250-ft multi-taped lift pioneered by the Royal Air Force Search and Rescue squadron in the Far East which made rescue possible from among trees 200-ft tall, too high for a normal winch cable to be used to reach the casualties. Once down, the engineers can have the landing area ready for the heavy helicopters in days or even hours.

The Bell AH-1G Hueycobra gunship of the US Army. The chin turret can be fitted with cannon, heavy machine-guns or grenade throwers, while a variety of weapons can be carried by the stub-wings.

The big helicopters have saved the lives of many civilians in threatened districts in Vietnam, evacuating whole villages, together with their food and even their cattle, pigs and chickens, from combat areas to safer zones. Although many aircraft have been destroyed on the ground by bombing and raids by the Viet Cong, a noteworthy feature of this war has been the number of both fixed- and rotary-wing aircraft that have been retrieved after being shot down. Chinooks have hauled numerous Hueys, Hughes, Cobras and others back for repairs, sometimes on board repair-ships, and in turn, many a

Chinook has been picked up by a Skycrane and returned for repair to fly again. It is claimed that the First Air Cavalry Division on occasion has had fifty or more helicopter casualties in a week and had most of them back in service within another week. One Hughes OH-6A was shot down, recovered, repaired and put back into service five times.

The US Air Force Rescue and Recovery helicopters, S-61s, known as Jolly Green Giants because of their green and brown camouflage, are said to have rescued thousands of airmen and more than a billion (US) dollars worth of damaged aircraft to be repaired for further service. Many of the rescued airmen are picked up by the special 250-ft jungle-penetrating hoist/cable.

But in one battle in 1968, pressed home in unfavourable weather according to one report, 140 helicopters were lost in a few days through collisions in clouds, hitting the tops of trees, or brought down by Viet Cong ground fire.

Total losses of helicopters officially announced by the US Department of Defense in June 1970 were 3,850 since 1961 in North and South Vietnam and the rest of South-East Asia. Of this total 1,704 were lost on combat missions and the other 2,146 because of accidents, operational hazards or ground attack.

The vulnerability of helicopters to small arms fire has been a somewhat controversial matter, in spite of the official American statement that during the first four years of helicopter support to Vietnamese forces only 48 were lost because of ground fire.

Helicopters going into assault either keep out of sight as much as possible by flying low and taking advantage of any cover, or keep out of range by flying at 2,000/3,000 ft or more and then drop down quickly over the target area to discharge troops and supplies. But it was realised during the Algerian war and other operations that they must be armed, not only for self-defence but to act as armed escorts for transport operations. Experiments began in the 1950s, and during the Vietnamese war whole new armament systems have been developed for the helicopter, together with technological advances in avionics and fire-control systems, especially during the past five years, which almost seem like science fiction. The term avionics is a contraction of aviation electronics and was devised to encompass the ever-increasing list of communication, navigation and flight control functions that are performed electronically.

Bell Iroquois (Huey) helicopters were armed in 1963, at first primarily with machine-guns and rockets, a pair of machine-guns and eight rockets on each side of the fuselage, or a system of 24 rockets a side. They proved so effective that the Bell company developed the two-seat twin-turbine Hueycobra which went into service in Vietnam late in 1967. It

This large twin-turbine single-rotor Sikorsky HH-53B long-range rescue helicopter is seen on its first flight on 15 March 1967. The inflight refuelling probe projects from the nose.

was the first helicopter to be designed solely as an aerial weapons platform.

Able to fly at about 200 mph, remain in the combat area longer than its predecessor and to carry more than twice the fire power, the Cobra has armour plating to protect the crew seats and the cabin sides. It has a gun turret under the nose that can be swivelled, elevated or depressed. In it is mounted a 'Minigun' which has six barrels firing in sequence at 6,000 rounds a minute. Stub-wings have mounts for pods of rockets, grenade launchers, anti-tank missiles or combinations of these and Miniguns.

A feature of the Cobra is its sleekness; the cabin is only 36 in wide which makes it easier to be hidden on the ground and harder to hit in the air – important assets for military operations.

The more sophisticated and bigger rigid-rotor Lockheed Cheyenne was intended as an Advanced Aerial Fire Support System for escorting the bigger transport helicopters and as a ground-attack aircraft. With a nose turret, full 360° swivelling belly turret, computer sighting for weapon firing, and able to carry a variety of anti-tank missiles and other weapons, it was to have gone into service in Vietnam. But difficulties during its development programme and the scaling down of the war in Vietnam caused the US Army to cancel its production order. With US Navy assistance Lockheed is continuing its test and development programme.

With conventional materials arming helicopters created problems, such as increasing weight, which meant augmenting engine power, not too difficult with uprated jet engines. Later special lightweight materials were developed for the armour plating and armament systems.

Avionics devices specifically developed for the helicopter, some of which are already in service in Vietnam, include terrain-following radar, light augmentation devices or low-level television especially suitable for night flying, a radar antenna concealed in the main rotor blade which it is said can

US Air Force Sikorsky CH-3C refuelling in flight from a tanker aircraft.

identify a truck at a distance of over a mile and moving tanks five miles away, computer-sighting for weapon firing, and the use of infra-red for target acquisition and identification.

War always stimulates technological progress, and it is to be hoped that many of these new devices, particularly those contributing to navigation and all-weather operation, permitting the pilot to fly by visual reference rather than by instrument procedures, will be available for the next generation of commercial helicopters.

	Rotor diameter	Length	Seats	Loaded weight	Cruising speed	Range
UNITED KINGDOM						
Westland Whirlwind*	53′ 0″	41′ 8½″ ⊖	12	7,500 lb	86 mph	300 miles
Westland Wessex 1†	56′ 0″	48′ 4½″ ⊖	19	12,600 lb	121 mph	390 miles
USA						
Bell UH-1B Iroquois	44′ 0″	39′ 7½″ ⊖	10	8,500 lb	126 mph	260 miles
Hughes OH-6A Cayuse	26′ 4″	23′ 0″ ⊖	4–6	2,400 lb	134 mph	413 miles
Sikorsky R-4B	38′ 0″	48′ 1″ =	2	2,540 lb	75 mph‡	130 miles

* British version of Sikorsky S-55
† British version of Sikorsky S-58
⊖ Length of fuselage excluding rotors
= Length including rotors
‡ Maximum speed

The Helicopter in Military Service [47]

6

The Helicopter at Sea

Just as air forces and armies were quick to realise the special qualities of the helicopter, so were navies round the world. The US Navy's first helicopter squadron was formed in 1946 and the first all-helicopter squadron to be formed outside the USA was commissioned by the Royal Navy in 1950 with the Sikorsky S-51 built under licence by Westland Aircraft and known as the Dragonfly.

At first naval helicopters were used for the usual duties, air/sea rescue, ambulance work, communications, transport and photography, but both American and British aircraft carriers with helicopters took part in the Korean war, flying in commando and marine troops. British carriers and their helicopters were in operation again during the 1950s when there were troubles in the Persian Gulf and in Malaya.

The potentialities of the helicopter in other directions were quickly realised and one of its most successful and important rôles since the early 1950s is in anti-submarine warfare (ASW).

Modern submarines have become much harder to attack and, as they can travel submerged at up to 30 knots, speed in attack is a vital factor. Because of its manoeuvrability, because it can hover and because it can travel up to five times as fast as a conventional ship and can change its position for search so much faster, the helicopter obviously has many advantages over the conventional ASW ship.

For ASW the helicopter is fitted with a winch-operated sonar (Asdic) set that, while the helicopter is hovering, can be lowered to very great depths in the water well below the water temperature layers that deflect the sonar signals. Because the helicopter is hovering little noise is recorded, which is important;

◀ A Westland Wasp, designed for all-weather anti-submarine operation from small landing platforms on destroyers and frigates. The ship is the *Tribal* class frigate HMS *Nubian*.

US Marines' Boeing-Vertol UH-46D Sea Knight making an approach
to land on the uss *Guadalcanal*

in a ship the sonar system is an integral part of the
ship's bottom and the water rushing past the sonar
and the noise from the ship's propellers can affect
adversely the efficiency of the system. In addition,
the sonar when lowered from a helicopter and
totally immersed to send out signals in the same
vertical plane, is not subjected to pitching and rolling
as a ship is during rough weather.

To perform these duties the ASW helicopter
carries one of the most complicated automatic,
electronic and computerised flight control and
navigation systems it is possible to imagine, and it is
all duplicated in case one part should fail. The flight
control system automatically controls speed, height
and heading to pre-selected values and maintains
the aircraft in level flight. The helicopter can be
flown manually but can also be flown on automatic
control from initial lift-off to positioning for landing,
controlling turns and transitions down to or up from
hover in accordance with pre-selections by the crew.
The automatic flight control system in all weather
conditions gives flight pattern accuracy that a pilot
could not possibly maintain.

The navigation system provides a position fix at
all times and a continuous display of information in
the pilot's cockpit. In the event of failure of any main
part a separate computer takes over to provide full
navigation information. In addition the helicopter
has all the radio, radar and homing facilities for
communications with its home base, ship or aircraft
carrier, and a telecommunication briefing system so
that the crew can be briefed while in the helicopter
on standby.

The normal crew of an ASW helicopter is four:
the pilot, responsible for the safety and control of
the aircraft, and his co-pilot, who fly the helicopter
and monitor its many automatic systems; the Anti-
Submarine Control Officer (ASCO), who is
responsible for navigation and co-ordination of the
whole search exercise and who has at his console a
presentation of all the relevant information on the

One of the Royal Navy's Westland Sea King twin-turbine multi-purpose helicopters developed from the Sikorsky S-61.
This type has an automatic flight control system and integrated sonar and search radar weapon system.

aircraft – height, speed, magnetic heading, navigation plot, as well as the sonar and radar presentation, and is also responsible for releasing the anti-submarine torpedoes or attack weapons; and the sonar operator who controls and operates the sonar under the command of the ASCO.

The ASW helicopter can be used to screen a convoy or task force as well as acting as a hunter/killer. When screening a convoy or task force it will only advance at the speed of the convoy so that the search is in the same relevant position to the force at all times, and in searching for and attacking known targets it will only remain in one position for as long as it takes to search that area. In this way the maximum amount of water will be searched in the shortest possible time. There are many different search patterns based on the number of helicopters available, the time factor, that is the time from which all measurements are made at the beginning of the search, and any other information, such as the type and speed of the submarine if this is known.

A typical ASW helicopter search would be on the following lines: the helicopter is hovering, heading into wind. The ASCO gives the order to go and the aircraft is climbed out of the hover to approximately 120 ft and 80 knots. This can be done automatically or manually. The helicopter is then turned on to a course, worked out by the ASCO, to bring the helicopter to the next search position and speed is increased to maximum cruise. At the correct time the aircraft is slowed to approximately 80 knots and turned into wind; on completion of the turn the helicopter is brought to the hover at approximately 40 ft, the sonar is lowered into the water to the required depth and the sonar search is started. When the search is finished the complete cycle is then repeated. When the sonar buoy is lowered to the required depth the range and bearing of the contact, or target, are displayed and then transferred to the radar display and the target speed is noted for plotting. The radar display also shows the position of any surface vessels in the area and the locations of any other ASW helicopters in the vicinity. Once the target is located it is attacked with appropriate weapons – homing torpedoes or even nuclear depth charges – and the helicopter returns to base under automatic control and under the guidance of its navigation and radar systems.

All the major navies of the world, and some of the smaller ones, use helicopters for ASW and other duties, and even the small ships, such as frigates of the Royal Navy, usually carry at least one of the smaller helicopters for ASW, transport, rescue work and as a link with other ships in the fleet. Search and rescue helicopters of the Royal Navy also co-operate, from shore stations, with local life-boats and coast guards on civil operations.

Traditionally, destroyers have been the anti-submarine ships of the navy. The US Navy has developed a robot helicopter known as DASH (Drone Anti-Submarine Helicopter) for use from the deck of a destroyer. Controlled by radar, it carries a homing torpedo and can be directed from the destroyer to the target.

At the beginning of 1970 it was estimated that the US Navy had some 1,600 helicopters and the Royal Navy well over 300 with approximately another 150 on order. The Soviet naval forces also use helicopters extensively and a new helicopter carrier is known to have gone into Russian service early in 1970.

7

Helicopter Airlines

In scheduled commercial operations the American helicopter airlines have contributed most to the development of commercial helicopters, operational techniques and heliports, although other countries, notably Belgium through its national airline Sabena and, in the United Kingdom, British European Airways, have added their contributions. BEA in fact operated the world's first 'sustained' passenger helicopter service – in 1950 – even though it lasted only ten months.

As early as 1946 the US Post Office Department inaugurated experimental helicopter air mail flights in three areas, Los Angeles, Chicago and New York. As a result, in 1947 Los Angeles Airways became the world's first scheduled helicopter air carrier, using four-seat Sikorsky S-51s and operating within a fifty-mile radius from the Post Office in downtown Los Angeles. Two years later Helicopter Airways (later Chicago Helicopter Airways) received a contract to serve an area within a fifty-mile radius of the Chicago Midway Airport, using two-seat Bell 47B helicopters. Both these companies operated daily flights from the roofs of the main Post Office buildings and both had outstanding safety records, Chicago Helicopter Airways making more than 40,000 roof-top landings and take-offs in its first two years.

New York Airways began helicopter air mail (sometimes called helimail) services with Sikorsky S-55s in December 1952, adding an air freight service for the scheduled airlines serving New York in January 1953, and in July that year carried its first passengers.

By November 1956 all three companies were

New York Airways began passenger services in July 1953, using Sikorsky S-55s but later introduced the bigger S-58s, one of which is seen here with flotation gear as it takes-off from West 30th Street Heliport on the Manhattan shore of the Hudson River.

operating scheduled passenger services between airport and airport, airport and city-centre and airports and the suburbs.

Chicago Helicopter Airways ceased operations in 1965 when Midway Airport was closed for re-building, but services between Midway and O'Hare Airports were resumed at the end of May 1969 with a fleet of ten helicopters, three Sikorsky S-58s, three

Bell 206As, three Bell 47Gs and one 47J. By the end of the year 4,000 passengers had been carried.

Until 1966 the US Government provided an annual subsidy for the helicopter airlines. When it was discontinued several of the major US trunk route airlines offered assistance, such as guaranteeing a quota of seats on certain helicopter flights, assistance in ticketing, reservations and advertising, and in leasing helicopters to them.

Today there are five main helicopter companies operating regular services in the United States – Los Angeles Airways, New York Airways, San Francisco and Oakland Helicopter Airlines, Chicago Helicopter Airways, and Air General which is operating within the Boston area.

By August 1970 Los Angeles Airways was operating about 150 flights a day between Los Angeles International Airport, one of the busiest in the USA, and a system of outlying heliports and airports serving twenty cities and communities directly and some 200 indirectly in southern California. Passengers, mail and express are carried on this unduplicated route mileage of 296 miles, mainly by Sikorsky S-61L 28-passenger twin-turbine helicopters, but on the longest route, 64 miles, de Havilland Twin Otter short take-off and landing aircraft carrying seventeen passengers have been used.

There are no scheduled services to downtown Los Angeles at present although the company is negotiating for a landing facility.

New York Airways is currently operating what they call a thirty-thirty service, that is a thirty-seat S-61 Mark II shuttle service every thirty minutes between New York's three main airports, Newark, LaGuardia and John F. Kennedy International. In the late 1950s the company operated regular services to and from the airports and a heliport on the Hudson River at West 30th Street in Manhattan but this was discontinued several years ago. After a period of operations at the Wall Street Heliport, in December 1965 the company operated passenger services from the roof of the Pan American building above Grand Central Station in mid-town New York to the John F. Kennedy Airport. Within the first three months some 2,000 passengers a day were using this heliport and in two years more than half a million passengers were carried, but this service stopped when the agreement between New York Airways and Pan American was not renewed. A new agreement was signed in 1970 and in May 1971 New York Airways resumed service to Manhattan using the Downtown Heliport near Wall Street. Service was also started to Morristown in New Jersey. During the interim period of eighteen months between the agreements with Pan American, New

York Airways operated de Havilland Twin Otter short take-off and landing aircraft, which they still had in 1970. In 1969 a total of 252,000 passengers was carried and since resuming helicopter operations in March 1970 load factors rose in two months from thirty per cent to fifty per cent – that is thirty and fifty per cent of the provided capacity was used.

San Francisco and Oakland Helicopter Airlines (SFO) is the only helicopter airline in the USA to have operated without a government subsidy and was the first to have an all-turbine fleet. It began services in 1961 with Sikorsky S-62s and received a permanent certificate of operation in 1963. In July 1970 about ninety flights a day were being operated between San Francisco International Airport and Oakland Airport, Berkeley, Marin County, Palo Alto and San Jose in California, with Sikorsky S-61N helicopters. These routes varied from twelve miles flown in about seven minutes to thirty miles in sixteen minutes. Passengers carried increased from 25,000 in 1961 to 325,000 in 1969.

Again there is the same sad tale of abandoned city-centre services. At one time SFO operated to heliports in San Francisco and Oakland but these flights were discontinued 'for various reasons', no doubt including the usual complaints of noise, and because of city development and encroaching buildings. For city-centre services the helicopter has as

yet certainly not achieved all that had been hoped but, on the present scale of operations, doubts of its ability to fit in with the air traffic control pattern for conventional take-off and landing aircraft at busy airports have been unfounded. Flying under the regular airlanes, they have not affected fixed-wing traffic whether operating under Visual Flight Rules (VFR) or Instrument Flight Rules (IFR) and they have been certificated for full instrument flight operations since 1966.

The United Kingdom also made early use of the special qualities of the helicopter, three RAF Sikorsky R-4s of the King's Flight making daily flights in August and September of both 1947 and 1948 carrying the King's mail from Dyce, Aberdeen, to Balmoral. During these two periods a total of 7,721 miles was flown. In May 1950 Westland Aircraft operated experimental passenger services in connection with the British Industries Fair, flying twice daily from Harrods Sports Ground at Barnes, a London suburb, to Castle Bromwich, Birmingham, with S-51s.

British European Airways established a Helicopter Experimental Unit in 1947 with three S-51s and two Bell 47Bs to explore the potentialities of the helicopter for scheduled operations. They began with mail and during the next three years operated for the Post Office several mail services, mainly in the Midlands, for short periods including one night mail service based on Peterborough. On 1 June 1950 they began the world's first regular passenger helicopter service, between Liverpool and Cardiff, followed a year later by one between London and Birmingham, and from July 1955 to May 1956 gave London a brief city-centre service from a site on the south bank of the Thames at Waterloo to London (Heathrow) Airport. This latter service was hampered by restrictions imposed by the authorities which included exhaust silencers, floats and a mandatory route up the Thames.

None of these services lasted and on the experimental routes in the Midlands especially traffic was poor. From 1956 the helicopter unit was kept busy with charter operations and continued government-sponsored development work which included much useful research on equipment and techniques for all-weather operations. In 1964 the airline formed BEA Helicopters Ltd and since May of that year has operated regular scheduled services between Penzance, Cornwall, and the Scilly Isles. They currently have a fleet of S-61Ns and one Bell Jet-Ranger and in 1969–70 carried more than 58,000 passengers. In addition, BEA undertakes contract charter work for the North Sea gas and oil prospecting companies, and since 1968, in co-operation with KLM Nordzee Helicopters NV, has been doing

◄ The Sikorsky S-51 played a part in developing helicopter passenger and mail services. This British European Airways S-51 is seen at Mudford in Somerset, England, in January 1948 during dummy mail trials.

contract work on the Dutch North Sea gas and oil explorations.

Within Europe, the Belgian state airline, Sabena, was the pioneer of scheduled helicopter operation, beginning in August 1950 and flying regular mail services with three Bell 47Ds. In 1953 passenger services were started and for a number of years Sabena operated a 230-mile circular route linking Brussels with eight other cities in Belgium. A shuttle service between Melsbroek Airport and a heliport in the centre of Brussels was also flown.

Later that year Sabena began the world's first international helicopter services on three routes linking Belgium with France, Germany and Holland. Seven-seat S-55s were used at first, and later, S-58s. In thirteen years 400,000 passengers were carried.

Throughout Sabena had financed these operations completely and, although they were not financially successful, continued to do so because they provided a valuable feeder service for its long-haul routes operated by fixed-wing aircraft. But in 1962, like most airlines at that time, the company was in financial difficulties and decided to discontinue its helicopter services, selling its fleet of S-58s to the Belgian armed forces. There were widespread protests from passengers and some of the cities served, and the company was persuaded by the Belgian Ministry of Transport to change its decision in

return for a subsidy. So, leasing two Vertol 44s from New York Airways, some of the routes were reopened but in 1966, after consultation with the Belgian Civil Aviation Authorities, the routes were again closed down on the grounds that there was no hope of them showing any profit in the foreseeable future. Today some of the services previously operated by the helicopters are flown by Fokker F.27 Friendship short-range propeller-turbine airliners.

The USSR, with its vast territories covering all varieties of terrain and climate, its comparative lack of roads and railways, and the vast distances to be covered, has made air transport its main communications system, although new railways and roads are also being built. Aeroflot, the state airline, is undoubtedly the biggest in the world and its use of helicopters exceeds that of any other nation. Although starting helicopter operations later than most of the other major countries, the Soviet Union began passenger services in the Crimea in 1958 and by the end of 1960 was understood to be operating more than one hundred scheduled helicopter services for passengers, mail and freight. These included services from the main central air terminal in Moscow to the three main civil airports around the city. Experiments were also made with mail services from the roof of the main Post Office building in Moscow.

◄ On 1 September 1953 the Belgian airline Sabena operated the first international passenger helicopter services, from Brussels to France and the Netherlands. This photograph, taken later, shows six Sabena Sikorsky S-58s departing from the Brussels heliport.

In the middle of 1970 it was reported that extensive plans, covering the next ten years, had been announced for extending helicopter services from Moscow to the outskirts of the city and to suburban areas. A number of new heliports in Moscow were to be situated near the city's underground stations. Mil Mi-8 thirty-seat helicopters were to be used and 600,000 passengers a year were expected to be carried.

In many other parts of the world helicopter airline services have been operated for some time. For the past ten years Ansett in Australia has been flying regular services in daylight between Essendon Airport and a heliport on the Yarra River in Melbourne, a distance of seven miles. The service is limited to weekdays only and carries about 2,500 passengers a year. A Bell 206A JetRanger has replaced the original Bell 47. Trans-Australia Airlines has also operated to the Yarra site. In addition, Ansett operates regular services with a Sikorsky S-61N from two airports on the mainland – Mackay and Proserpine – to four of the main island tourist resorts on the Great Barrier Reef, as well as tourist flights to other islands and over the actual barrier reef. Services in this area are subject to seasonal fluctuations and cover distances varying from 23 nautical miles – Proserpine airport to South Molle Island – to 69 nautical miles from Mackay airport to Hayman Island. Cyclone

Ada in January 1970 caused a temporary interruption of these services.

In Italy Elivie (Societa Italiana Esercizio Elicotteri), which was ninety per cent owned by Alitalia – the national airline – operated regular helicopter services from Naples to some of the nearby islands for nearly fifteen years. Originally on a seasonal basis, later there were regular year-round services from Naples to heliports at Capri, Ischia and Sorrento/Positano, but operations ceased early in 1971. A fleet of S-61Ns, Agusta-Bell 204Bs and Jet-Rangers was used.

Greenlandair (Groenlandsfly A/S) was formed in 1960 but did not begin operations until 1963. Since then it has flown scheduled services from Godthaab to nine centres in Greenland with S-61Ns and an Alouette III. Coastal ice patrols are also maintained and, in addition, the company operates a fleet of fixed-wing aircraft in support of USAF operations in Greenland and Eastern Canada.

In Japan two companies operate extensive services – All Nippon Airways, with a fleet of twenty-three helicopters, and Japan Domestic Airlines. The latter, which was formed in 1964 by the merger of several Japanese domestic companies, has a fleet of fifteen helicopters, mainly Japanese-built, and operates secondary domestic and feeder routes. All Nippon Airways' fleet includes one S-55, two

During 1963 Pakistan International Airlines began developing a network of helicopter services in East Pakistan. This PIA Sikorsky S-61N is seen at Sandwip on the Dacca–Chittagong route.

Alouette IIs and a number of Kawasaki-Bell 47s and KH-4s. JDA became Toa Domestic Airlines in 1971.

A valiant attempt was made by Pakistan International Airlines in 1963 to operate regular services to some of the more inaccessible parts of East Pakistan with S-61s but after four years, and the loss of one helicopter and other difficulties, the services were abandoned. In 1970 the company investigated the use of short take-off and landing aircraft to reopen some of the former helicopter routes and has acquired a fleet of Twin Otters.

Olympic Airways for the past two or three years has been operating limited services to some of the Greek islands with Alouette helicopters, and for a time operated the large French Super Frelon.

Scheduled helicopter services are costly to operate and have maintenance difficulties but there is still widespread interest in them and in 1970 there were reports of two new possible centres of operation. In Hongkong Hutchison International Ltd was formed to operate regular services to Kai Tak Airport from a helipad at Harcourt Road near the centre of Hongkong; and in Western Canada, the Calgary Transportation and Development Authority announced plans for helicopter taxi services between a heliport on a river site in the downtown area of the city and the airport.

	Rotor diameter		Length		Passengers	Loaded weight	Cruising speed	Range
FRANCE								
Aérospatiale Super Frelon	62′	0″	63′	$7\frac{3}{4}''$*	34–37	27,557 lb	143 mph	108 miles
ITALY								
Agusta-Bell AB-204B	48′	0″	40′	$4\frac{1}{2}''$*	10	7,500 lb	124 mph	279 miles
USA								
Sikorsky S-55	53′	0″	42′	2″*	8–10	6,835 lb	90 mph	440 miles
Sikorsky S-58	56′	0″	46′	9″*	16–18	13,000 lb	98 mph	280 miles
Sikorsky S-61N	62′	0″	72′	10″*	30	19,000 lb	140 mph	115 miles
Sikorsky S-62	53′	0″	44′	$6\frac{1}{2}''$*	10	7,900 lb	92 mph	270 miles
Vertol 44B†	44′	0″	86′	4″	15	14,350 lb	101 mph	90 miles
Vertol 107†	50′	0″	44′	7″*	25	19,000 lb	150 mph	115 miles

* Length of fuselage excluding rotors
† Tandem rotors

8

Heliports

Special landing and take-off areas for helicopters are known as heliports; in the USA, which probably has more than any other country with the exception of the USSR, they are called helistops or helipads if no facilities such as fuel or maintenance are available. Most other countries just refer to them as heliports or landing pads.

Heliports are usually at ground level or on top of roofs. In the USA, however, there is another category – elevated, which usually means some 100 ft above the ground. This may be an oil drilling rig, a deck over a car park, or the roof of a large garage or a six to ten-storey hotel. It can also be at an industrial site or a transport centre which links and co-ordinates bus, rail, car and helicopter traffic in one convenient location near the main centre of the city and the main highways. Work on one such centre is well advanced at Pomona, California.

The ground-level heliport is considered to be the most practical at present and is the most widely used everywhere. Whether at ground level or elevated, heliports need to be clear of nearby obstructions and to have good approach and departure paths; this is even more necessary for elevated ports.

The size of a heliport or landing pad area varies tremendously. For commercial airline operations the minimum size is considered to be at least 200 ft by 400 ft and, unless they are allocated areas at major airports, they are usually fenced in. Most heliports have perimeter lighting and even the smallest will have at least a wind direction indicator and some form of firefighting equipment. A typical oil rig landing pad would be about 60 ft square and some 100 ft above the water.

In the USA the minimum size for a hospital roof-top landing pad or helistop, adequate for small helicopters, is 25 ft by 25 ft and is usually on a load-distributing pad to spread the concentrated loads over the existing structure. Most helistops, especially roof-top ones, are for the two/six-seat helicopters operated for private use and by police for traffic and crime control, by newspapers, banks and so on. They range from 40–50 ft to, on the ground, 100 ft by 100 ft or more. Municipal heliports are larger and may be square, rectangular or circular. The area of the heliports/helistops obviously depends on the size of the helicopters using them and the density of helicopter traffic, but for safety and for the helicopter to be able to manoeuvre there should be space on the approach and over the landing area to give a clearance of at least one third of the overall diameter of the rotor blades.

A large white circle or a 32 ft triangle is usually painted at the spot where the helicopter is to land and sometimes an H is painted in the centre which gives the pilot a useful guide to how much room he has to manoeuvre. Elevated and roof-top ports often have a number painted on them, for example eleven, which indicates a weight capacity of 11,000 lb.

Eventually international standards for marking heliports and landing pads may be required, particularly if the use of helicopters in co-operation

This photograph, taken in February 1961, shows a New York Airways Vertol 44 landing at the New York Downtown Heliport near Wall Street.

with merchant shipping is extended, as seems extremely likely.

The most famous roof-top heliport is the one on top of the Pan American World Airways building in central Manhattan. This was opened in 1965, in connection with the New York World Fair, and services were flown between it and the heliport on top of the Port of New York Authority's building at the Fair. The latter had a landing area of 150 ft by 200 ft at an elevation of 120 ft, but the top of the Pan Am building is 800 ft above ground level with a landing area of 121 ft by 113 ft. Services were operated successfully to and from the World Fair and later to New York's airports but operations from the Pan Am building have now ceased.

There are special problems in operations from pinnacle heliports, as they are sometimes called in the USA. Stringent noise and safety regulations imposed by the regulatory authorities are one main reason why many ground level heliports in cities are situated by the riverside, and these factors are even more important in built-up city centres, imposing severe restrictions on approach and departure flight paths. Airflow around very tall buildings is another source of trouble – even at ground level, as pedestrians in many cities have discovered in recent years. This was overcome on the Pan Am heliport by placing metal vanes on all edges of the roof to smooth out the flow of air crossing the roof, but even so in taking-off and landing turbulence could be experienced from other nearby skyscrapers.

Instrument approach and guidance systems (ILS) are now routine for all helicopter airlines but opera-

tions to the Pan Am building were restricted to Visual Flight Rules (VFR) – that is, when adequate visibility is available. At the time, the ILS equipment was too big to be accommodated on the Pan Am building and, because of the uneven heights of surrounding buildings, would have given uneven signals. The increasing reliability of twin-engined gas-turbine powered types, and the revolutionary advances made in Vietnam with instruments and landing aids for military helicopters, have made it possible for pilots to fly with television devices by visual reference rather than instrument procedures, in which case downtown pinnacle heliports may increase. Ground supporting devices such as beacons and transmitters would no longer be necessary, which would make landing much simpler and safer.

A somewhat surprising feature of the Pan Am heliport operations was that despite its situation in mid-town New York it was found that not everyone wanted to go to that particular part of the city centre. Coming from other parts of the mid-town area, passengers found that to use a taxi direct to the airport, in spite of road traffic, was faster than using a taxi to the Pan Am building, getting to the top and going by helicopter to the airport.

Opinion now is that three or four heliports in different parts of a big city, with good parking facilities and near other forms of transport and main

The Port of New York Authority's West 30th Street Heliport in Manhattan was used by New York Airways' services to the New York airports. One of the airline's Sikorsky S-55s is seen on the landing pad close to the small terminal. A second pad is out of the picture to the right.

highways, will be more useful than one main city centre heliport. Also, that as the cost of building and

servicing a heliport over about 100 ft elevation rises sharply, this height is a good compromise.

In addition to the heliport on the roof of the Pan Am building in Manhattan, New York has had two other heliports which were used by helicopter services. The first was the West 30th Street Heliport beside the Hudson River. This had two landing pads over the river, a taxiway between the two, and a small terminal. The second New York heliport was on the East River near Wall Street and was constructed on one of the city's piers. There is a single landing pad and a taxiway linking it with the roadside terminal.

If the next generation of helicopters each carry 80 to 100 passengers, as seems likely, the size of heliports will have to be increased, and this will be simpler at ground level or over large parking centres.

The Anaheim/Disneyland heliport in California claims to be the world's busiest. Los Angeles Airways, operating some 26 round-trip flights a day to and from the heliport and Los Angeles International Airport, carried its millionth passenger to Anaheim on 19 August 1969. The flight time is sixteen minutes; by road, even expressway, the journey would take more than an hour. The heliport is at ground level, is fenced in and occupies an area of 400 ft by 180 ft. It has free parking for more than 250 cars. Not only is Anaheim the home of the world-famous Disneyland

The Westland Heliport London, over the Thames at Battersea, was opened
in April 1959 and night flying began there in 1960.

but it has also become a popular centre with special facilities for conventions.

According to the Aerospace Industries Association of America at the end of 1968, the latest date for which statistics are available, there were 1,812 heliports/helistops in the USA of which 1,734 were at ground level and 158 were elevated; of these only 48 were specifically described as roof-top. As this overall total was 600 more than in 1966 and the number of heliports/helistops has been increasing steadily, there must now be well over 2,000. The 1968 total did not include some 300 heliports and more than 5,000 helistops around the USA maintained by the US Forest Service. In addition, there were more than a hundred offshore oil rig landing pads in the Gulf of Mexico alone.

A Trans-Australia Airlines' Bell 47J helicab on the landing pad over the Yarra River in Melbourne in 1962.

At the same time Canada had a total of 73 heliports/helistops, only one of which was elevated.

The first British heliport to be used by regular passenger services was Haymills Rotorstation near Birmingham. This was used by BEA's Sikorsky S-51s which began operating a London Airport Heathrow – Northolt Airport – Birmingham service in June 1951. This continued until April 1952 when a cargo helicopter service was introduced between the London and Birmingham *airports*. Haymills Rotorstation consisted of a small fenced area in which there was a wooden passenger terminal and two small circular landing pads. BEA also used a number of heliports for subsequent services, including one on the site of the 1951 Festival of Britain near Waterloo Station, close beside the Thames over which the single-engined S-55 helicopters were forced to fly.

In 1970 the United Kingdom had three licensed heliports, all at ground level. They were the privately-owned and operated (since 1959) Westland Heliport London on the Thames near Battersea with a landing area of 125 ft by 53 ft and restricted to helicopters with an all-up weight of 36,000 lb; the BEA Helicopters' civil helicopter site at Gatwick Airport which is 500 ft by 475 ft; and the BEA Penzance heliport which has a landing pad 100 ft by 100 ft in the centre of a strip some 900 ft by 150 ft.

Early in 1970 two more heliports were proposed for London, both on the River Thames: a temporary site in the St Katherine's Dock Development Area which it was hoped would be in service by the end of the year (it was not) and, by early 1972, a 300 ft by 80 ft floating platform near Waterloo Bridge. The British Helicopter Advisory Board is advocating the provision of a number of heliports in many parts of the country, including elevated ones in city centres as new and quieter helicopters become available.

In Belgium a number of heliports were constructed to handle that country's domestic air mail service which began in August 1950. Then when international passenger services began in September 1953 a large heliport was constructed near the railway terminus at Allée Verte in the centre of Brussels as well as heliports in other cities including Lille and Rotterdam. The Brussels heliport had a terminal building with customs facilities and a long taxiway leading to the 65 ft square landing pad. Six helicopters have been operated at this heliport at one time.

Pakistan International Airlines built several heliports for its services in East Pakistan. These were small fenced areas with modest terminals, radio facilities, and hardstandings for the helicopters. At Chittagong, near the Burma border, the landing area was on top of a small hill and was made of bricks, which resulted in the helicopters taking-off in a great cloud of dust and stones which smothered the hundreds of onlookers who watched every arrival and departure.

Another city-centre heliport is the small one above the Yarra at Melbourne. This is just large enough to take one small helicopter and is connected to the terminal by a sloping gangway.

There are heliports all over the world, the bulk of them at ground level, although the Soviet Union has at least one elevated one in Moscow.

9

Workhorse of the Air

Wherever there are earthquakes, hurricanes, floods, disasters of any kind in any part of the world, the helicopter will be in action, rescuing people, flying in food, medicines and other supplies. In the devastating earthquakes in Peru in 1970 a Boeing CH-47C Chinook of the US Army sighted a hundred children and fifty adults stranded in a small village up in the mountains and managed to load them all aboard and fly them out to safety. This is but one example of the many wonderful performances of the helicopter in saving lives since the first recorded medical mission by the US Coast Guard on 3 January 1944. The US Coast Guard also devised the hoist method of rescue. It is estimated that well over 100,000 lives have been saved by American-built helicopters alone.

Many countries, including the United Kingdom, rely on the helicopters of their military services for civilian ambulance and search and rescue operations, but in the USA the Coast Guard Service and State police forces are general watchdogs, and many business operators, private owners and helicopter taxi operators provide general services to their local communities as required.

Much of the work by helicopters can be – and often is – done by light fixed-wing aircraft, tasks such as agricultural spraying and dusting, fish spotting, aerial taxi work, to mention only a few, but the ability of the helicopter to hover and to land where other aircraft cannot makes it unique.

Although more expensive to operate than fixed-wing aircraft, helicopters are used extensively in agricultural work, especially in the USA, USSR and Japan as well as in Australia and New Zealand, two

The helicopter has played an enormous part in saving lives. Here a French Sud-Aviation Alouette II is rescuing the crew from the bows of the *Silver Valley* off Portugal in March 1963.

other pioneering countries in this field. They are used for spraying chemicals and fertilisers, for treatment of the soil, for plant nourishment and for pest control.

They can save crops in other ways, too. Flying over orchards, the downwash from the rotors is used to remove the frost from citrus fruits, and valuable cherry crops have been saved by blowing raindrops off the fruit. The helicopter's downwash has also brought a breeze to yachtsmen becalmed ahead of dangerous squalls, and has blown stranded boats off sand bars. Helicopters have towed ships of over 300 ft in length and weighing 3,000 tons.

Helicopters have also been used – experimentally – to spray oil slicks with a special new chemical, the downwash from the rotor agitating the surface of the sea and speeding up dispersal of the slick.

In the USA on large ranches helicopters are used to herd cattle, ride the range, patrol fences, and it is said that one can do the work of fifteen cowboys. They have also been used in various parts of the world for assessing the bird and wild life populations within particular areas.

An unusual – and hazardous – wild life rescue operation was undertaken in South Africa in September 1970. Helicopters of the South African Air Force uplifted more than 200 rare crocodiles, some weighing over 1,000 lb, from the salt-poisoned waters of a lake in Northern Natal to a freshwater lake some fourteen miles away. It was a particularly dangerous operation as the crocodiles, starving because their staple diet of freshwater fish had died, had first to be rounded up into open water by rangers in water-jet-propelled skiboats. The rangers then had to cast a large nylon hammock net over each crocodile so that the hovering helicopter could winch it up and fly it to its new home.

In logging operations helicopters hover over inaccessible places in forests, drop crews where they are required, and pick up the lumber when it has been felled and haul it to roadside areas to be loaded aboard trucks. High operating costs preclude extensive use in this way at present, but early in 1969 that downwash of the rotor blades proved invaluable again when logging operations on Vancouver Island were held up because of particularly heavy falls of snow – an unusual occurrence in that part of Canada. Snow ploughs cleared the roads so that loggers could get to the trees, but as soon as they tried to use their saws down came masses of snow and branches made brittle by the freezing temperatures. The answer was a call to the mainland and the arrival of helicopters to blow the frozen snow from the trees. 'Operation Downdraft', as the company called it, was a complete success and logging production was resumed with confidence.

Another method of rescue. A Royal Canadian Air Force Boeing-Vertol 107
makes a rescue from the surface of the water.

Helicopters also help with forest fire-fighting – flying in foresters, water containers, directing operations on the ground; and again sometimes using downwash from the rotors to blow the smoke away and to help divert the course of the fire. Later they help to renovate devastated areas by seeding.

Hospitals are making increasing use of helicopters for emergency cases, or to rescue people injured in bad traffic accidents, especially on busy American highways, where a helicopter can often get an injured person to hospital much faster than a road ambulance. At the end of 1969 four states in the USA were undertaking, with federal assistance, an experimental programme of emergency medical services for highways. By 1970 some 250 hospitals in the USA had their own helipads. West Germany has also instituted a Helicopter Medical Emergency Service for road accidents.

Banking would not usually be connected with helicopters but – again in the USA – a number of

A Soviet Kamov Ka-26 with outrigger spray-bar for agricultural work.

banks are using helicopters to collect from their suburban branches cheques, mail and other items needing processing and deliver them to the main bank so that they can be cleared overnight. They may use roof-tops, lawns, and parking lots for these operations or, in some cases, pole pick-ups such as trains once used to collect mail from small stations without stopping. One of the US banking companies making extensive use of helicopters in this way around the San Francisco area, but operating from designated heliports, is Wells Fargo, a name well known to all Western film fans.

Most people are familiar with the search and rescue work of the helicopter saving yachtsmen in difficulties at sea, or sailors from foundering ships, climbers – or skiers – in mountainous regions, or crashed aeroplanes from mountains or forests, but they play an important rôle in many lesser-known activities. These include whaling; geological, topographical, mining and seismic surveys; archaeological surveys – discovering possible sites often shown up from the air, especially from variations in crop marks which indicate interesting possibilities and which cannot be seen from the ground; supplying lighthouses and weatherships; exploration of jungles, deserts, forests; photographing volcanoes; fish spotting – directing fishing fleets to areas where shoals of fish have been located; and for observation of movement of icebergs. The USSR uses helicopters for ice floe reconnaissance and on its drift stations in the Polar regions. Most ships used for Arctic and Antarctic survey and exploration now carry at least one helicopter.

Helicopters are also used by many police forces not only for traffic control purposes but for crime control. The Paris Préfecture de Police uses them for special patrols, riot control and traffic observations; in the United Kingdom many trucks now have identification marks on the roof to help police helicopters to locate them if they are stolen. Helicopters have also been used during the troubles in Northern Ireland.

In the Philadelphia area of the USA motorists can tune in to fourteen radio stations for accurate up-to-date reports of traffic conditions based on helicopter observations. In Lakewood, California, a day and night helicopter police patrol, known as 'Project Sky Night', was inaugurated in 1966. The police helicopter is never more than $2\frac{1}{2}$ min away from any part of the city. Special, portable high-intensity lights, capable of floodlighting an area as big as a football field, are carried, with business men and householders co-operating by installing flashing lights on roof-tops which can be switched on in emergency. Project Sky Night is said to have proved a very real deterrent to criminal activity, robberies in the area dropping by 22·5 per cent during the first twelve months.

Recently a light-weight searchlight has been produced for fitting to helicopters such as the Bell 47 for police, fire and rescue units and other organisations needing high-intensity lighting in the field.

In Italy the Carabinieri (police) have been using a combination of police dogs and helicopters for fighting crime in some parts of the country and for mountain rescue. Special containers for the dogs were developed to be carried on each side of the helicopter.

Smugglers of anything – diamonds, drugs, gold, people, tobacco – may find the helicopter an enemy because there are anti-smuggling helicopter patrols in many parts of the world. There is a nice story from Denmark – in the summer of 1969 a tobacco smuggler's boat was chased by a helicopter, the whiplash, or downwash, from the rotor pursuing him from the open sea and finally cornering him in a dead-end canal in Copenhagen.

Have you a house to move? Not long ago a (literally) round house some 25 ft in diameter, designed in Finland and built in Sweden, was delivered by train to its owner in Stockholm but the problem was to get it to its final destination. The Swedish Air Force with a Boeing-Vertol 107 helicopter lifted it from the railway car and deposited it gently on its steel foundation at its home site.

The helicopter is now being widely used as a crane, as already shown by mention of it retrieving crashed aircraft in Vietnam and by the lifting of the house in Sweden. Power-lines have been laid by helicopters after they have lifted the pylons into position, and crosses have been positioned atop church towers and steeples.

Production of the crane helicopter was one of the most important developments and one with a great potential. Although the USSR with the Mil Mi-6 and its developments the Mi-10 and now, much bigger, Mi-12 far outstripped the Western world both in helicopter size and weight-lifting capacity, it is

A French Sud-Aviation Djinn carrying a slung-load while working in the Antarctic.

interesting that in the USA the Russian-born Igor Sikorsky had been thinking along similar lines for the helicopter for some time. The Mi-6 made its first flight in the autumn of 1957 and the first Sikorsky crane some eighteen months later.

The Skycrane was largely Sikorsky's own creation. He had reached retirement age in 1957 but remained as a consultant to the company, and long before then he had talked of a crane helicopter which would have no limitations on the bulk of the loads it would carry; he even described what it would look like. Sketches drawn by his son Sergei were published in the January 1958 issue of *The Bee Hive*, the quarterly magazine of the United Aircraft Corporation of which Sikorsky Aircraft is a division. Those sketches were prophetic, showing the sort of jobs Sikorsky foresaw would be done by the new aircraft, such as lifting sections of bridges, houses, radar towers, bulldozers and other construction equipment.

When it flew for the first time, on 25 March 1959, the S-60, as the research prototype was designated, bore a strong resemblance to those early sketches. A bigger version and the first production Skycrane, the S-64, made its first flight in May 1962 with two 4,050 shp Pratt & Whitney gas-turbines mounted side by side on top of the fuselage boom. It did not look at all like any previous Sikorsky helicopter. The S-64 has no conventional fuselage; instead a long, slender boom extends from the top of the pilot's cabin back to the tail rotor. Below the boom there are the hoist and hardpoint attachments and space for carrying all kinds of external cargo, including trucks, and special containers or pods incorporating a field hospital unit, or space for 48 casualty litters, 67 troops or 22,890 lb of cargo. The S-64 also has a landing gear that can be lengthened or shortened hydraulically depending on the load to be carried.

The S-64 and the Soviet Mi-10 bear a superficial resemblance to one another but where the S-64 has a boom from the pilot's cockpit the Mi-10 has a cabin fuselage for passengers, troops or additional cargo.

The first S-64 Skycranes went into service with the US Army in 1965 and the first two commercial examples, the S-64E, have been operating on the North Slope of Alaska since 1969 with Rowan Air Cranes, carrying up to ten tons at a time to remote oil drilling locations.

Whereas the Sikorsky Skycrane has a swivelling seat for the co-pilot to enable supervision of loading and unloading, the Mil Mi-10 has a cockpit panel with a closed-circuit TV screen on which the external loads and touch-down of the main undercarriage are monitored. The Mi-10 also has a huge undercarriage which can straddle bulky loads, such as a 32-seat bus on a pre-loaded platform. A second version, the Mi-10K, with short undercarriage legs and apparently intended mainly for construction work, has a small cabin with a backward-facing seat and controls for a pilot to handle the aircraft and operate the hoist.

10

Commercial Operators

At the end of 1969 well over 5,000 helicopters were being operated by some 800 companies and individuals in more than a hundred countries around the world, not including the USSR and certain Eastern European countries. At least one half of these were in the United States and were American-built. Some 600 companies in the USA now use a helicopter like a company car to transport executives and customers between factories and airports; the rest of the operators are private owners, charter firms (hire firms), air taxi firms, or companies performing under contract many of the duties of the helicopter already described. The number of companies using helicopters for general duties is growing in all parts of the world, although the number using fixed-wing aircraft for general aviation, as it is called, is still greater. Canada, France, the United Kingdom,

Germany and Japan come next to the USA in numbers of helicopters operated.

In most forms of construction work helicopters have proved their worth, not only in carrying equipment and personnel to difficult or inaccessible places, but in the saving of time, labour and money. At one time some construction work was an arduous, time-consuming business, especially in places where there were no roads. Now helicopters not only fly in people, supplies and equipment but, as previously mentioned, actually do some of the work, such as setting into position poles and towers for electrical power-lines and then stringing the cables. They can do as much work in a few hours as would take three to four days by normal means. Lifting heavy steel beams to the tops of buildings under construction, placing them exactly where needed, pouring wet

◀ An Okanagan Helicopters' Hiller 12E hovers on a Canadian mountainside to discharge men and supplies.

concrete for foundations, lifting the final span of a bridge into position, putting spires on top of cathedrals – a helicopter put the flèche (as it is called) on top of Coventry cathedral in 1961 – these are some of the jobs done by helicopters. When power-lines are laid helicopter crews undertake inspection work, not only of electrical power-lines but of oil pipe-lines. In the United Kingdom in 1967–68 two Hiller 12E helicopters of the Central Electricity Generating Board were used in making maintenance inspection flights over 9,000 miles of overhead power-lines in two and a half weeks – a job that would have taken foot linesmen two years or more.

Another field of activity for helicopters, and one that is likely to increase, is in connection with merchant shipping. A commercial operator is already providing a service at Cape Town which is used by many vessels rounding the Cape. Using, at present, single-engine helicopters, about 1,000 lb of mail and stores are winched down by the helicopter while hovering over the deck of the ship. The US Navy is using helicopters to supply carriers and other ships while at sea with provisions, mail and even aviation fuel, in an operation known as 'vertical replenish-ment'. There are possibilities for transferring crews and cargo, loading and unloading, to or from ship and shore by helicopter in areas where there are no docking facilities or where the size of the ship and tidal conditions make the use of existing docking facilities difficult. This can be done by the helicopter winch (a kind of small crane), for small freight packages, or by the external hoist with cargo under-slung or again, using the big crane helicopters. This would seem to have possibilities for container ships, to enable complete containers to be delivered en route where no special container terminals are available, and experiments have already taken place. The USSR has been using the big Mi-6 to load and unload ships at sea ports and on rivers for several years.

For the Western world the hire of the helicopter would obviously be expensive but if docking time for large ships could be reduced or, in some cases eliminated, shipping companies would make an overall saving on costs. New merchant ships of the future may well include provision on their decks for landing areas for helicopters.

In Alaska, where there is now intense activity with new oil finds at North Slope, Prudhoe Bay, crane helicopters have moved a complete drilling rig, more than 1,000 tons of equipment, in nine days over the tundra which in summer is waterlogged. This is another major undertaking for helicopters round the world: oil drilling and natural gas exploration, not only in Alaska but in the Middle and Far East, Africa, the Americas and the North Sea.

A BEA Sikorsky S-61N picking up a load from a lorry at Battersea Heliport before flying across the Thames to position it at the power station.

The North Sea is one of the biggest areas of oil and natural gas exploration in the past five or six years, where British, Danish, Dutch, German and Norwegian firms are operating together with helicopter companies under contract to them. The North Sea looks, on a map, as if it were small and sheltered; it is one of the most heavily travelled shipping routes, and one of the most treacherous, its 280,000 square miles of water being noted for their tidal currents, sudden changes of weather and, at times, almost impossible flying conditions. Yet commercial helicopter-operating companies are serving offshore oil- and gas-rigs anything up to 150 miles from bases in the United Kingdom, Scandinavia, Holland and Germany.

The three biggest commercial helicopter companies in the world, always excepting the Soviet Aeroflot, are Bristow Helicopters of the United Kingdom, Okanagan Helicopters of Canada and Petroleum Helicopters of the USA.

Bristow Helicopters was formed in 1951 as Air Whaling by Alan Bristow who learned to fly the Sikorsky R-4B helicopter in 1944 while serving with the Royal Navy. In fact he pioneered the use of helicopters for whaling in the Antarctic and extended his operations to offshore drilling in 1955, at first in the Persian Gulf, Nigeria and the Caribbean, and then in the North Sea. Today Bristow's company operates some 130 helicopters – mainly Alouette, Bell 47, Hiller and Westland types – from thirty bases in twenty countries through twelve associate companies. Their work is now mainly under contract to the oil and natural gas industries, and consists of ferrying men, supplies and equipment between shore bases and offshore rigs. Bristow helicopters have been responsible on several occasions for saving crews on drilling rigs and well-heads (production platforms), especially in the notorious North Sea. Bristow also operates a training school in the United Kingdom, and since 1963 has been responsible for training all British Army Air Corps pilots.

During its almost twenty years the company has undertaken practically every task performed by helicopters, except scheduled passenger-carrying. Yet it has carried more than 400,000 passengers.

Okanagan Helicopters, with headquarters at Vancouver, was originally founded in 1947 and has a number of subsidiary companies in Canada. In July 1970 it had a fleet of 44 helicopters comprising fifteen Bell 206As, two Bell 204Bs, twelve Bell 47 series, ten Hiller 12Es, three Sikorsky S-55s, one S-58, and one S-61. Its operations include transport; forest protection (firefighting) – both crew support and water bombing; mining exploration – moving crews and supplies to remote and inaccessible areas; construction projects, power-lines, pipe-lines; Arctic

oil exploration; and operations in support of oil-rigs offshore and oil exploration. The S-61 is used for these latter duties, and the S-58s and Bell 204Bs mainly in major explorations, construction of power-lines and forest protection. Probably some of its most important work has been construction duties and exploration work in the rugged territory of British Columbia and Northern Canada. It has also operated in Labrador.

Okanagan's helicopters fly more than 30,000 hours a year out of twelve bases in British Columbia and of the 150 or so permanent employees about fifty are pilots. Altitude and operating conditions make all mountain operations outstandingly difficult (because of reduced engine performance and turbulent air) and in the far North there is an extremely short operating season. Because so much of the work is in these rugged areas Okanagan Helicopters operates a special mountain-flying school. It is situated in the mountains where temperatures can get down to well below zero, winds can be forty mph and more and the mountains are over 8,500 ft high, with canyons, flat fields, forests, narrow rock walls and up to 800 ft projections of rock, with up and down draughts of air. Operating in regions like this calls for very special skills and concentration in flying and Okanagan finds sometimes that even experienced pilots with several thousands of hours of helicopter flying do not make the grade in the last ten hours or so of altitude flying. The school has such a high standard and record that graduates are exempt from the Canadian Department of Transport's checks.

Through its subsidiary companies, Okanagan has pioneered and developed much special under-slung equipment for fire-fighting, agricultural spraying, cable line stringing, and special cargo hooks for carrying multiple loads, as well as an automatic remote hook which can pick up an external load without assistance from ground personnel while the helicopter hovers.

Petroleum Helicopters, with headquarters in Louisiana and a fleet of 140 helicopters, claims to be the world's largest and most experienced helicopter operator. Founded in 1949, it has from the beginning been particularly interested in offshore oil operations in the Gulf of Mexico but today operates as well in Canada, Alaska, Africa, and most of South America where at one time it used a Soviet Mi-10 crane. The company operates about 150,000 flight hours a year and handles some 30,000 passengers a month.

In Louisiana oil workers use the helicopter as a bus to their daily jobs on the oil-rigs anything from fifty to a hundred miles or more out in the Gulf of Mexico. The company has also specialised in construction work which has included missile sites in the USA, radar stations in the Arctic, pipe-lines in South America and mining in Indonesia.

In the early days of commercial helicopter operations it was said that jobs had to be thought up for them to do; that certainly does not apply today. Who knows what else they will be used for in the future?

11

Today's Helicopters

Several countries have designs for small helicopters, including the Argentine, Denmark, Indonesia and Poland, and Poland builds the Soviet Mil helicopters and India the French Alouette IIIs; but the main countries designing and building helicopters today are France, the German Federal Republic, Italy, Japan, the United Kingdom, the USA and the USSR. All can trace their interest in and contributions to the development of rotary-wing aircraft back into history, but for most there was a gap during the 1939–45 war and work on helicopters was not generally resumed until the late 1940s and early 1950s.

In the past twenty years there have been changes in many of the world's aircraft constructors through reorganisation, mergers and take-overs. A type originally designed by one company may have been developed by another and end up by being produced and marketed by yet another, which does not help for clarity.

This chapter describes the more important helicopters now in production or under development. They appear alphabetically by countries and within these sections alphabetically under the names of the companies currently producing or developing them. During their working lives helicopters, like fixed-wing aircraft, are subject to development, and variations are introduced, such as different engines, different equipment, which result in changes in weight, range and performance; the figures given in the tables therefore should be considered as typical of the type only.

◀ The world's largest helicopter, the Soviet Mil Mi-12 with twin rotors, four 6,500 hp turbines, and a weight of more than 100 tons.

FRANCE

France began designing and building helicopters again soon after the end of World War II and in the past twenty years has produced a number of successful types, notably the Alouette (Lark) II and III, and versions of these, and the Super Frelon (Super Hornet). They have been used by all the French armed forces and have been sold in numbers to more than thirty countries.

Best known of the French helicopter companies in recent years has been Sud-Aviation which was formed in 1957 by the amalgamation of two companies which, in their turn, had been created in 1936 by the nationalisation of private companies. Now Sud-Aviation has become part of another consortium – Aérospatiale (Société Nationale Industrielle Aérospatiale). Under an Anglo-French agreement signed in 1967 the SA 341 Gazelle all-purpose lightweight and SA 330 Puma medium-size transport helicopters are being built for the British and French forces. Design leadership is retained by France.

The company also has under development an ultra-light VTOL vehicle, the Ludion, intended to carry one man, his personal equipment, and a payload of 66 lb for several hundred yards at a height of some 500 ft.

The following were the main types in production in 1971:

	Rotor diameter	Length	Seats	Loaded weight	Cruising speed	Range	Duty
SA 318C Alouette II	33′ 5⅝″	31′ 11¾″⊖	5	3,630 lb	112 mph	186 miles	General purpose
SA 316B Alouette III	36′ 1¾″	32′ 11″⊖	7	4,630 lb	118 mph	186 miles	General purpose
SA 321 Super Frelon*	62′ 0″	63′ 7¾″⊖	32	27,557 lb	143 mph	400 miles	Heavy duty
SA 330 Puma	49′ 2½″	46′ 1½″⊖	18	14,110 lb	165 mph	380 miles	Transport
SA 341 Gazelle	34′ 5½″	31′ 2¾″⊖	5	3,750 lb	152 mph	425 miles	Multi-purpose

⊖ Length of fuselage

* Numerous versions exist for a wide range of duties including transport and anti-submarine work.   All these helicopters are Aérospatiale designs

A French Navy Aérospatiale Super Frelon powered by three 1,550 hp turbines. A passenger version was used for a time by Olympic Airways on services between Athens and some of the Greek islands.

GERMAN FEDERAL REPUBLIC

During the past fifteen years or so since independent operations began again in Germany, that country's aircraft industry, as elsewhere, has undergone a number of changes and only one of the old names remains – Dornier. This company has had more

experience in VTOL civil aircraft with the Do 31 deflected thrust and direct jet lift technique than any other, and has a proposal for a 100-seat aircraft for military and civil operation before the end of the 1970s.

Dornier has also been building under licence the American Bell UH-1D for all the German forces for various duties including search and rescue and frontier policing. In addition Dornier has had under development a single-engined four/six-seat single-rotor light multi-purpose helicopter, the Do 132, with a two-blade tip-driven rotor.

The most interesting of the recent German helicopter projects is the Bölkow Bö 105 light utility five/six-seat project with a rigid rotor and four-blade main rotor made of glass-fibre reinforced plastics. This is being built by Messerschmitt-Bölkow-Blohm. Initial flight tests of the rotor were made on the French Astazou-powered Sud-Aviation Alouette II, but the first prototype was destroyed and the second flew early in 1967.

Germany also has under development the Wagner Sky-Trac I, with contra-rotating rotor system, and the Aerocar. The first of these is intended mainly for agricultural duties. The second is a four-seat helicopter with an enclosed cabin, and with rotor blades which fold back for road use.

The highly successful turbine-powered Bell 206A JetRanger utility 4/5-seat helicopter. It has a maximum speed of 150 mph.

	Rotor diameter		Length		Seats	Loaded weight	Cruising speed	Range	Duty
Messerschmitt-Bölkow-Blohm Bö 105	32′	1¾″	28′	0½″*	5/6	4,410 lb	143 mph	373 miles	Light civil and military
Dornier Do 132	35′	1¼″	24′	7″	5	3,152 lb	137 mph	275 miles	Multi-purpose
Wagner Sky-Trac 1	32′	9¾″	23′	3½″	1	3,300 lb	87 mph	125 miles	Multi-purpose
Wagner Aerocar	32′	9¾″	—		4/5	3,300 lb	—	—	Roadable helicopter

* Excluding main rotor

ITALY

Three companies in Italy are building American helicopters under licence – Agusta, the Bell and Sikorsky types; Meridionali, the Boeing-Vertol Chinook; and Nardi, the Hughes 500. In addition, SIAI-Marchetti in co-operation with Silvercraft is building the SH-4 helicopter. Most important of these companies is Agusta (Costruzioni Aeronautiche Giovanni Agusta SpA) originally established in 1907. Agusta acquired a licence to build the Bell 47 helicopter in 1952 and has since built variants of the Bell Model 47, the Bell Iroquois, JetRanger and Sikorsky SH-30 Sea King for the Italian armed forces. Agusta-Bell helicopters have been exported to many countries. In addition, Agusta has developed special variants of the series Bell 47 of its own design and has also produced its own designs for the Italian services. Apart from the USA and USSR Agusta has probably built more helicopters than any other concern.

The basic American designs are given in the USA tables, and the original Agusta types hereunder.

	Rotor diameter	Length	Seats	Loaded weight	Cruising speed	Range	Duty
Agusta A 101G	66′ 11″	66′ 3″⊖	38	27,340 lb	124 mph	264 miles	General purpose
Agusta A 106	31′ 2″	26′ 3″⊖	1	2,954 lb	104 mph	150 miles	Anti-submarine
Agusta A 109C	36′ 1″	35′ 1½″⊖	8	5,070 lb	155 mph	388 miles	Light transport
SIAI-Marchetti/ Silvercraft SH-4	29′ 7½″	25′ 1¼″⊖	3	1,900 lb	80 mph	200 miles	General purpose

⊖ Length of fuselage

JAPAN

After the ending of the Pacific war Japan was not allowed to build aircraft, but following the conclusion of the Peace Treaty in 1952 the Japanese aircraft industry was quickly reorganised and aircraft production began.

Comparatively little original helicopter work has been done in Japan but numbers of United States designed helicopters have been built under licence by Japanese companies and there have been Japanese developments of some of these types.

Fuji Heavy Industries, successor to Nakajima who built about 30,000 aircraft up to 1945, has produced numbers of Bell 204B and UH-1B helicopters and supplied them to the Japan Ground Self-Defence Force, to All Nippon Airways, Japan Domestic Airlines, the Tokyo Police and even to the Bell Helicopter Company in the USA. Fuji also added small wings to a UH-1B as an experiment in relieving the flight loads on the rotor.

Kawasaki, an old-established aircraft manufacturer, developed the KH-4 from the Bell 47G and put it into quantity production, selling numbers in Japan and exporting the type to Thailand, Korea, Burma and Brazil. Kawasaki has built more than 500 Bell 47s and KH-4s. From the KH-4, Kawasaki developed the experimental KHR-1 with rigid rotor and flew it for the first time in April 1968. Kawasaki also has exclusive rights to build and sell in Japan the twin-engined tandem-rotor Boeing-Vertol 107 Model II which is known in Japan as the KV 107. This type is produced in a number of versions, both civil and military, and most have been sold in Japan but one was supplied to New York Airways, and two were sold to Pan American Airways for operation by New York Airways. Kawasaki also builds the Hughes 500 light helicopter.

Mitsubishi, another famous name in Japanese aviation, holds licences from Sikorsky for the manufacture of the S-61, S-62 and SH-3A types, numbers have been produced and some exported to other Asian countries.

Main details of these types are given in the table following the United States section of this chapter.

The Sikorsky S-61L landplane and S-61N amphibian were chosen by a number of airlines. This amphibious example is seen in the livery of Ansett-ANA, now Ansett Airlines of Australia.

UNITED KINGDOM

The United Kingdom's connection with helicopters goes back to Sir George Cayley in the eighteenth century and contributed to the success of the Cierva Autogiros. Interest in the 1920s and 1930s was mainly concentrated on the Autogiro, a number of which were built by A. V. Roe and Co (now submerged in the Hawker Siddeley Group) and by the Scottish firm G. & J. Weir Limited which was closely associated with the Cierva company.

Weir built two helicopters in the late 1930s but

their development was stopped by the 1939–45 war. The company took over Cierva, although it retained its original name, and in 1949 produced the Air Horse, at that time the largest helicopter in the world; it crashed the following year and its development was not continued. Cierva also designed the little two-seat Skeeter, but in 1951 the Cierva company was taken over by Saunders-Roe which later became part of the Westland group of companies. The Skeeter finally went into service in 1957 with the British Army and the Royal Air Force and a small number were also used by the Federal German Army and Navy.

For some years after the Second World War helicopter design and production was concentrated in three main companies – the Bristol Aeroplane Co, Fairey Aviation Co and Westland Aircraft.

In 1944 the Bristol Aeroplane Company took over the AR III Construction (Hafner Gyroplane) Company which had been formed by Raoul Hafner after he came to England from Austria in 1933. The company had built one or two successful machines and during the war Hafner designed an ultra-light rotary-wing glider known as the Rotachute which could be launched from an aircraft. It was technically successful, but it did not go into service. With Bristol, Hafner was responsible for design of the two-seat Sycamore (Type 171), the first Bristol type and the first British helicopter to receive – in 1949 – a certificate of airworthiness. They were used by the Royal Air Force, the British Army, Royal Australian Air Force and Navy, British European Airways, Belgium, and Federal German forces.

Various other Bristol designs followed, including the 173 Belvedere, the United Kingdom's first twin-engined tandem-rotor helicopter design, which made its first free flight in 1952. Originally intended for the Royal Navy it was taken over by the Royal Air Force and, capable of carrying 18–25 fully-equipped troops or twelve stretcher cases, it was still in service in the Far East in 1968.

The Fairey Rotodyne should be mentioned because it was an advanced compound helicopter which made its first vertical flight in 1957 and set up a speed record of 191 mph in 1959. Both civil and military versions were planned and aroused much interest but in 1962 its development was finally abandoned because of lack of government support. Ironically, more than one design produced in other parts of the world in the past six or seven years has born strong resemblance to the basic outlines of the Rotodyne.

In 1960 all helicopter activities in the United Kingdom were merged in Westland Aircraft who continued work on two designs originally begun by Saunders-Roe as replacements for the Skeeter.

The Sikorsky CH-53 Sea Stallion can carry 38 fully-equipped troops or 12½ tons of military stores.

These were the Scout and Wasp. The Scout (single Blackburn Nimbus engine) was a five-seat general purpose helicopter which went into service with the Army in 1963. A number were also exported, two being used by the Royal Australian Navy for ship-borne survey work. The Wasp (single Nimbus engine) was designed primarily to operate from the rear decks of frigates and went into service with the Royal Navy late in 1963. Some have also been sold to other navies.

Westland began a long association with the Sikorsky company in 1947 when it acquired a licence to build the four-seat S-51 in the United Kingdom. Known as the Dragonfly it saw extensive service with the Royal Air Force and the Royal Navy. The S-55 was the next to be built, the British version being named Whirlwind; it was used extensively by the Royal Air Force, the Army and the Navy, and a number of civil versions with up to eight seats were also built. The Series 3 Whirlwind was a turbine-powered version which served extensively with the British military services; a commercial version was also produced and two served with the Queen's Flight. A number of the earlier Whirlwinds were returned to the makers for conversion to turbine power.

In 1956 Westland acquired the licence for the Sikorsky S-58 and it was produced as the Wessex Mk. 1 with a single Napier Gazelle turbine. As the first British turbine-powered helicopter, it went into production for the Royal Navy in 1959 as a submarine search and strike helicopter. Later versions of the Wessex had two coupled Rolls-Royce - Bristol Siddeley Gnome turbines and were delivered to the Navy and the Royal Air Force, and a number were sold overseas. Seven Wessex Mk. 60s (equivalent to the Wessex Mk. 2) have been built for Bristow Helicopters Limited as ten-seat passenger aircraft; they are used in connection with oil and gas drilling rigs in the North Sea.

The fourth Sikorsky design to be built by Westland was the SH-3D Sea King (derived from the S-61B) which was designed from the beginning as an Anti-Submarine Warfare helicopter for the US Navy, and which went into service in 1966. With two 1,500 shp Gnome engines and all-British equipment, the Sea King, in service with the Royal Navy, is claimed to be the most advanced and powerful anti-submarine weapon in service anywhere. It has power-operated automatic folding blades. Considerable interest in the Sea King has been shown by several countries.

Westland is also involved in the Anglo-French agreement, originally signed in 1967, for three types of helicopter for the armed services of both countries. Design leadership of two of the types – the SA 330 Puma assault helicopter, already in production in France, and the SA 341 Gazelle light observation helicopter, the prototype of which is flying, rests with France – originally Sud-Aviation, now Aéro-spatiale (SNIAS). Design leadership of the third type, the WG.13 Lynx, rests with Westlands. It made its first flight early in 1971. A utilitarian helicopter with semi-rigid rotor, it is intended for the British and French Navies, the British Army and for commercial operations. Considerable use is being made in its construction of some of the new materials such as carbon-fibre laminates. Interest is being shown in the civil possibilities of the Lynx, and the US Navy is understood to be considering it for its light airborne multi-purpose system (LAMPS) helicopter requirement, in which case Sikorsky would probably have the licence to build.

Westlands also have a 100-seat VTOL project, the WG.22, based on a convertible-rotor design.

The table opposite gives the leading particulars of Westland helicopters in production in 1971, or under development.

	Rotor diameter		Length		Seats	Loaded weight	Cruising speed	Range	Duty
Westland Wessex 50/60[1]	56′	0″	48′	4½″⊖	12/18	13,600 lb	121 mph	334 miles	Transport
Westland Sea King[2]	62′	0″	55′	9¾″†	4*	21,500 lb	131 mph	1,105 miles †	Anti-submarine/transport
Westland Wasp HAS.1	32′	3″	30′	4″⊖	2/5	5,500 lb	110 mph	270 miles	General purpose
Westland Scout AH.1	32′	3″	30′	4″⊖	2/5	5,300 lb	122 mph	315 miles	General purpose
Westland WG.13 Lynx	42′	0″	38′	3¼″⊖	14	8,000 lb	184 mph	506 miles	General purpose

[1] UK development of Sikorsky S-58   ⊖Length of fuselage   † Ferry range
[2] UK development of Sikorsky SH-3D   ⁺ With rotors folded   * In the transport rôle the Sea King can carry 27 troops

UNITED STATES OF AMERICA

The practical helicopter was developed in the United States and the pioneer work of Igor Sikorsky, which led to today's helicopters, is related in Chapter 2.

More types of helicopter have been designed and built in the United States than anywhere else. The outstanding names in US helicopter design are those of Sikorsky, Bell, Piasecki, Boeing-Vertol, Lockheed, Hiller, Kaman, and, more recently, Hughes, but there have been many others associated with rotary-wing development.

Sikorsky have developed the helicopter from the early two-seat R-4 up to the present S-61 civil and military series, the big S-64 Skycrane, S-65 Sea Stallion, and the very fast S-67 Blackhawk gunship which has flown at more than 220 mph.

Bell designed the very successful Model 47 which, in various forms, has been in continuous production since 1946 with well over 5,000 built in the United States and under licence in other countries. Bell have never gone in for the very big helicopter but have undertaken steady development of the classic Model 47 design and produced such outstanding types as the Model 204/205 Iroquois, Model 209 Hueycobra gunship, the twin-turbine Model 212, and the Model 206 JetRanger which is in large-scale production.

Frank Piasecki played an important part in the development of the tandem-rotor helicopter and it was his designs which were taken over and de-

The big twin-turbine Sikorsky S-64 Skycrane which can carry a variety of loads attached to or slung from its slender rear fuselage.

veloped by the Boeing-Vertol concern, leading to the Vertol 107 airliner, the Sea Knight military development and the much larger Chinook – all twin-turbine tandem-rotor helicopters.

Lockheed was much later in turning its attention to helicopters. The company built the experimental Model 186 and 286 with rigid rotors and these proved to be fast and have aerobatic capability. Then Lockheed's Cheyenne gunship design won the 1966 Army design contest for an advanced aerial fire support system. This type had a four-blade rigid rotor, small fixed wings and a retractable undercarriage, but the Cheyenne encountered trouble during its test programme and was cancelled.

Hiller produced a series of small single-rotor helicopters and now under the title Fairchild Hiller the company is producing the FH-1100 turbine-powered four/five-seat utility helicopter.

Kaman was founded in 1945 and much of the company's work has been devoted to design and construction of helicopters with intermeshing rotors, but the current production Kaman helicopter, the US Navy's HH-2C Seasprite, is an orthodox twin-turbine single-rotor type which is both armed and armoured and mainly used for search and rescue. Under development by Kaman are the K-700 general purpose helicopter with twin-turbines and intermeshing rotors, and the K-800 gunship with single four-blade rotor and small fixed wings.

The Hughes Tool Company's Aircraft Division has been involved in the design of both small and very large helicopters but all its production helicopters have been small and highly manoeuvrable. Main production is centred on two types, the Model 300 and Model 500. Several versions of the two/three-seat Model 300 exist, including a trainer, and quite large numbers have been built. The Model 500 is a dainty single-rotor helicopter with egg-shaped cabin having up to five seats. In service with the US Army as a light observation type, the Model 500 is known as the OH-6A Cayuse.

Main details of these United States helicopters are given in the following table and because of the wide range of designations frequently given to the same basic design, this section ends with a designation list of the principal US helicopters.

	Rotor diameter	Length	Seats	Loaded weight	Cruising speed	Range	Duty
Bell 206A JetRanger	33′ 4″	31′ 2″⊖	5	3,000 lb	122 mph	362 miles	General purpose
Bell 209 Hueycobra	44′ 0″	44′ 5″⊖	2	9,500 lb	166 mph	362 miles	Gunship
Boeing-Vertol CH-46 Sea Knight*	50′ 0″	44′ 10″⊖	28	21,400 lb	150 mph	230 miles	Assault transport
Boeing-Vertol CH-47 Chinook*	60′ 0″	51′ 0″⊖	47	37,700 lb	172 mph	250 miles	Transport
Fairchild Hiller FH-1100	35′ 4¾″	29′ 9½″⊖	5	2,750 lb	122 mph	348 miles	Utility helicopter
Hughes 300	25′ 3½″	21′ 11¾″⊖	3	1,670 lb	80 mph	300 miles	Light general purpose
Kaman HH-2C	44′ 0″	37′ 8″⊖	2/13	12,585 lb	152 mph	340 miles	Search and rescue
Sikorsky S-64 Skycrane	72′ 0″	70′ 3″⊖	3/5	42,000 lb	109 mph	253 miles	Crane
Sikorsky CH-53A Sea Stallion	72′ 3″	67′ 2″⊖	41	35,000 lb	173 mph	257 miles	Assault transport
Sikorsky S-67 Blackhawk	62′ 0″	64′ 3½″⊖	2	18,496 lb	186 mph	—	Multi-purpose gunship

⊖ Length of fuselage
* Tandem rotors

Details of the Bell UH-1B Iroquois and Hughes OH-6A Cayuse appear on page 47, and of the Sikorsky S-61N, Sikorsky S-62 and Vertol 107 airliner on page 62.

Bell Model 47	USAF UH-13
	US Army OH-13 and TH-13T
	US Navy TH-13 (formerly HTL)
	British Army Sioux A.H.Mk. 1 and 2
Bell Model 206	
JetRanger	US Navy TH-5YA SeaRanger
	US Army OH-58A Kiowa
Bell Model 204	US Military UH-1A/B/C/E/F/L,
	HH-1K and TH-1F/L Iroquois
Bell Model 205	US Military UH-1D/H Iroquois
	Canadian Military CUH-1 Iroquois
Bell Model 209	
Hueycobra	US Army AH-1G
	US Marines AH-1J
Boeing-Vertol 107	US Navy and Marines CH-46/UH-46
	Sea Knight
	RCAF CH-113 Labrador
	Canadian Army CH-113A Voyageur
	Swedish Military HKP-4
Boeing-Vertol 114	US Army CH-47 Chinook
Hughes Model	
300	US Army TH-55A
Hughes Model	
500	US Army OH-6A Cayuse (formerly HO-6)
Kaman Seasprite	US Navy UH-2 (formerly HU2K-1) and HH-2
Kaman K-600	US Navy HOK-1
	USAF HH-43 Huskie (formerly H-43)
Sikorsky S-58	US Navy LH-34 and SH-34 Seabat
	US Army CH-34 Choctaw
	US Marines UH-34 and VH-34 Seahorse
	British Wessex
Sikorsky S-61	
Series	US Military RH-3 and SH-3 Sea King, VH-3A, CH-3B
	Canadian Navy CHSS-2
	Royal Navy Sea King
Sikorsky S-64	
Skycrane	US Military CH-54
Sikorsky S-65A	US Navy CH-53A Sea Stallion
	USAF HH-53B/C
	US Marines CH-53D

◀ The very advanced Sikorsky S-67 Blackhawk armed helicopter which in 1971 set a speed record in excess of 220 mph – then the highest helicopter speed to be officially recorded.

THE USSR

The Soviet Union's interest in helicopters goes back many years. Apart from Sikorsky's two unsuccessful attempts in 1909 and 1910, another designer, Yuriev, is said to have obtained a patent in 1911 for a helicopter with a single main rotor and a torque-balancing tail rotor, which was unsuccessful.

During the 1920s and for the next twenty years some research on rotary-wing aircraft was undertaken and several types were built and flown, but helicopter development was given low priority until several years after the Second World War. Then production was concentrated on two main design centres, those of Nikolai I. Kamov and Mikhail L. Mil. The Kamov types employ the co-axial contra-rotating system and large numbers have been built for multi-purpose duties with the armed forces and for agricultural and other work.

Mil designs until the latest have all had the single main rotor and anti-torque tail rotor. They are of particular interest because they are capable of carrying heavier loads than any others. Mikhail Mil (who died in 1969) was quick to take advantage of the shaft-turbine engine and used it first in the Mi-6 (1957) which for about ten years was the largest

The large Soviet twin-turbine Mil Mi-6, seen here with stub wings and, on the fuselage sides, auxiliary fuel tanks.

helicopter in the world, a distinction it then shared with its developments the Mi-10 and Mi-10K.

More recently an even bigger type has been produced, the Mi-12. This vast helicopter, by far the biggest in the world, made its first public appearance, outside the Soviet Union, at the 1971 Paris Air Show. The Mi-12 differs from previous Mil designs in having two rotors.

The very deep fuselage, which can carry a load of 40 tons and transport an assortment of vehicles, has clamshell rear loading doors and a ramp. Mounted in the high position are inversely tapered wings at the extremities of which are pairs of 6,500 hp Soloviev D-25VF turbines – each pair driving a five-blade rotor of the type used in the Mi-6 and Mi-10. The rotors are contra-rotating and it is believed that the port and starboard rotors are linked in case of complete failure of one pair of engines.

The Mi-12 has an orthodox aeroplane tail unit with fixed fin and rudder and horizontal tailplane and elevators. There are trimming surfaces on the trailing edge of the wing. This new type will cruise as a compound helicopter with a proportion of the lift being provided by the fixed wing.

The hold dimensions are approximately 92 ft 4 in in length by 14 ft 5 in in width and height.

Already the Mi-12 has set a number of international records including the lifting of an 88,634 lb load to a height of 7,380 ft. Normal take-off weight is 213,848 lb (presumably with vertical take-off) and maximum take-off weight is 231,485 lb. At this higher weight a rolling take-off would almost certainly be used.

Soviet helicopters have been sold to Albania, Afghanistan, Cuba, Finland, India, Pakistan, the United Arab Republic, and the Soviet bloc countries, and several types have been built under licence in Poland and China.

The table below gives the main details of the principal Soviet helicopters in 1971.

	Rotor diameter	Length	Seats	Loaded weight	Cruising speed	Range	Duty
Kamov Ka-25K	51′ 7¾″	32′ 3″ ⊖	10	15,652 lb	105 mph	400 miles	Transport and crane
Kamov Ka-26	42′ 7¾″	25′ 5″ ⊖	2/8	6,966 lb*	62 mph	215 miles	Multi-purpose
Mil Mi-4	68′ 11″	55′ 1″ ⊖	10/18	15,983 lb	99 mph	320 miles	Transport
Mil Mi-6	114′ 10″	108′ 10¼″ ⊖	68/103	89,287 lb	155 mph	650 miles	Transport, firefighter, crane
Mil Mi-8	69′ 10¼″	60′ 1″ ⊖	34	24,471 lb	125 mph	223 miles	Transport
Mil Mi-10	114′ 10″	107′ 9½″ ⊖	3/31	95,791 lb	111 mph	155 miles	Transport and crane
Mil Mi-10K	114′ 10″	107′ 9½″ ⊖	3/4	83,776 lb	155 mph	185 miles	Crane
Mil Mi-12**	114′ 10″	121′ 4¾″ ⊖	6/256	231,485 lb	150 mph	—	Heavy lift, 40 ton payload

⊖ Length of fuselage   * Agricultural dusting version   ** Side by side rotors

12

The Future

As traffic on roads becomes more and more congested and as airports and airways around the major cities of the world become more and more choked, in the USA and Europe especially, attention is being turned increasingly to the problem of general short-range transport. That in three or four years' time the supersonic transport (SST) may fly from London to New York in about three hours and from London to Sydney in about twelve, but that passengers will take an hour or even more from the centre of their home city to get to the airport before starting their air journey, is farcical.

In many cities today it has been said that lorries and cars move more slowly than the horse-drawn carts of sixty years ago, certainly in rush hours. In the middle 1950s it was estimated that a New York–Chicago air passenger spent a third of his time in ground transit; more recently it was nearly half. For some years the time spent in the air between London and Paris has been less than that spent on the ground getting to the airports.

Car parking at major airports is already a problem. At Toronto International Airport it is chaotic in spite of a vast multi-storey car park immediately opposite the terminal building; and travellers approaching Los Angeles International Airport have been warned over their car radios that all parking lots were full. Underground car parks may be one solution, for a time, but they are expensive to build. At least one airport in the USA is now providing off-airport parking for staff and taking them to and from their work by bus. The very large jets such as the Boeing 747 are already arriving at airports with 300 or more passengers at a time. And what if, as has already been forecast, even bigger jets carrying anything up to 1,000 passengers arrive? The situation on the ground will become even more chaotic.

The larger aircraft may slow down demands on Air Traffic Control with one aircraft carrying the loads of two, three or four of today's airliners, but the bigger the aircraft the stronger the runways needed for them. Even if they do not need longer runways, runways and taxiways may have to be widened for the really big aircraft because of the increase in undercarriage wheelbase; larger wing spans will require bigger parking aprons and the increased heights of aircraft will mean the provision of new loading facilities. The door of the Boeing 747 is 17 ft from the ground compared with the 10 ft 6 in of the Boeing 707. Handling facilities and services for such large groups of passengers and their luggage will need more and more automation. The 747 has special containers for luggage and freight, a practice which will doubtless grow, but it also needs special handling equipment. At the end of 1968 the British Airports Authority estimated that the new gates, air jetties, assembly areas and terminal facilities for the 747 and its successors at London Heathrow would cost over £12 million.

The current forecast is that by 1978 the London area will be faced with handling some 850,000 aircraft movements and 45 million passengers a year. In the USA it has been estimated that the total number of air passengers at 22 major cities there, which was 140 million in 1965, will be 740 million by 1980.

One of the first airports designed from the beginning to cope with the big new jets is Roissy-en-France, fifteen miles from the centre of Paris. It covers 7,500 acres and is due to be in operation in 1972, yet the French themselves feel that if air travel grows as it is forecast, Roissy will be in danger of saturation by 1985.

Is there a solution to this problem? Not just more and bigger airports, obviously. The controversy in the United Kingdom over the siting of a third airport for London is a good example of the feeling of the public. Apart from the availability of land no one wants a big airport with its noise on his doorstep, while airport authorities, airlines and passengers want a site as near the city as possible and with good, quick approaches to it.

During the past year or two more and more attention has been given to two possible solutions – vertical take-off and landing (VTOL) and short take-off and landing (STOL) aircraft. The latter is a fixed-wing aircraft with special aerodynamic features that provide high lift and good control at slow speeds. Once it touches down on a runway it can be stopped quickly and it can take off after a short run. A STOL aircraft cannot take off vertically, it cannot hover and it needs more clear airspace than a helicopter, but it is less complicated and cheaper to build and operate. It can operate from runways of 1,500 ft to 2,000 ft instead of the 8,000/12,000 ft needed by the big jets.

A number of small STOL aircraft, such as the Canadian DHC Beaver and Twin Otter, are already in service and have indeed been used on occasion by some of the helicopter airlines.

Airport, airways and ground congestion could be relieved by the establishment of small airports for short-haul air services, costing far less and occupying 150 acres, say, instead of the 4,000 or more (in some cases ten or more square miles) needed by a major airport. Such smaller areas could be easier to find near big cities and, if situated near trunk roads or passenger train links, could speed up transport greatly. A site of this type is under consideration by the Port of New York Authority which operates New York's three major airports and its heliports. Additional heliports at ground level on the water front in New York are also proposed.

That the airport is not the final destination of a passenger but just an intermediate stop *en route* to his business appointment or his home has now been realised. Three or four heliports at ground level, or

elevated to a height of 100 ft perhaps, in different parts of a city, or three or four small airports in urban areas with fast connecting links to the city would, it is believed, be more useful than one radial airport as well as relieving congestion.

The helicopter was the first of the VTOL aircraft, but so far the early dreams of its advocates that it would provide the universal solution to operations in and out of cities have not been achieved. This is mainly because of the helicopter's high operating and maintenance costs, noise, and at present, limited speed, range and carrying capacity. Initially single-engine operation and the problems of safety, hazards of navigation, noise and congestion in the approach areas, imposed strict limitations on city-centre operations, but even with the greater reliability of the helicopter over the years, and multi-engine operations, authorities are still strict with their requirements.

The problem of noise is not confined to the helicopter; it applies to most aircraft – usually on take-off and landing – and as the public becomes more noise-conscious and restrictions on operations, particularly at night, become more stringent, designers everywhere are working on the problems of suppressing noise and producing quieter engines.

Before the end of the 1970s new helicopters, possibly compound ones, carrying up to a hundred

A variation on the helicopter principle. This LTV XC-142A can take-off vertically by swivelling its wing so that the propellers act in the manner of a helicopter's rotor.

people and able to fly faster, equipped with some of the new avionics equipment developed for military aircraft, should be available. There are designs for compound helicopters using rotors for take-off and landing and fixed wings and propellers for forward flight; in some cases the rotors are folded and stowed when the aircraft is flying horizontally. There is also the Lockheed rigid-rotor compound helicopter (described in Chapter 3) which the company is continuing to develop.

The first of a new generation of VTOL aircraft to go into production and into service is the British Hawker Siddeley Harrier strike/reconnaissance fighter. The Harrier has thrust deflection nozzles which direct the exhaust power of its engine downwards for take-off and landing and aft for horizontal flight. Harrier units are to have a number of helicopters to provide back-up service in the field.

Other VTOL concepts include the tilt-wing in which the wing and engines tilt upwards for take-off and landing; the lift-fan system whereby the engine exhaust drives fans buried in the wings and fuselage for take-off and landing, the exhaust being redirected and the fans covered for forward flight; and another design which uses one set of engines for vertical and descending flight and another set for forward flight.

Several countries are working on the V/STOL aircraft, including no doubt the Soviet Union. The United Kingdom and West Germany have projects for 100-seat city-centre airliners, the British types intended for service in 1982–83 but the German one proposed for 1977. The Dornier company in the German Federal Republic has had a small VTOL experimental airliner, the Do 31, flying successfully since 1968. This has two vectored turbofans and, in addition, two removable packs of five lift-jets mounted at the wingtips and has a speed of over 400 mph.

The slowing down of the war in Vietnam and the financial difficulties being experienced by many countries nowadays, together with the ever-increasing costs of research and development, may lead to a slowdown of work on new projects. Nevertheless within the next ten to fifteen years new types of VTOL aircraft will be flying and decisions should be made soon on terminal sites for them if they are to be available when required. Far-reaching planning decisions are being taken in many principal cities in the Western world, and sites for Vertiports, as

they will probably be called, should be allocated and preserved now, with all their requirements borne in mind, even if they are not built for several years.

This will need consultation with the planners, city authorities, airline operators and designers of prospective VTOLs. Some of the heliports established in the USA even fifteen years ago can no longer be used by the more modern helicopters because of the unplanned building of industrial estates, and the expansion of residential areas and other buildings around the heliport.

Although helicopter airline operations have shown so far that they can operate in the same airspace as conventional aircraft without interference, an increase in VTOL operations, with the newer types operating at higher speeds and heights in already congested air lanes, will call for new airways and add to air traffic control problems.

Helicopters and all other types of VTOL aircraft will have to face increasing competition from the ground in the form of the advanced passenger train (APT), such as Japan's Tokaido Express, which operates every twenty minutes in the rush hours between Tokyo and Osaka, a distance of 320 miles, travelling at speeds of up to 130 mph.

Special very fast trains using existing railway tracks are under consideration in several countries, and in France, the United Kingdom and the USA entirely new concepts operating on the air cushion vehicle principle (a craft which rides on a cushion of air over land or water) are being developed. Electric linear induction motors which are quiet, economical in operation and maintenance are being suggested for these new trains. Two French companies already have experimental trains under test and in the United Kingdom the tracked hovercraft operating on an easily constructed elevated track was expected to be ready for test by the end of 1971. Intended for speeds of 150/300 mph and carrying a hundred passengers, it would be especially suitable for city-centre to airport services or on short-range routes of up to 500 miles between cities.

By the year 2000, provided that nations have the money to spend and the problems are thought to be sufficiently important, there may well be a complete revolution in transport based on the long-range SST and high-capacity wide-body jets, medium-range airliners, V/STOL types and helicopters, advanced passenger trains, and for water routes hovercraft and hydrofoils. There may even be automated highways and computer-controlled or electrically operated cars.

At one time helicopter enthusiasts were predicting that the time would come when everyone would fly his own small helicopter. This might not be impossible; if the demand were great enough costs would come down very much. Interest in small helicopters and autogyros is growing and there have been several new ones on the market recently. The number of helicopters used by private owners and firms is increasing and will probably continue to do so – at the end of 1969 there were 2,586 in the USA – and although many people in America use small helicopters as they would a car, with their own helipad on the roof of their garage, a sky full of small helicopters is a frightening thought.

The helicopter is assured of a place in world transport for many years to come but the final words on its future should be those of Raoul Hafner. Born in Austria, he built his first helicopter in 1927 and since 1930 has worked in the United Kingdom and contributed much to British rotary-wing aircraft, designing first for the Bristol Aeroplane Company and later for Westland Aircraft.

In 1969 Raoul Hafner wrote a series of papers entitled *The Second Century* which were published by the Royal Aeronautical Society. In one of these, on *The Future of Rotorcraft*, although he thought that eventually the pure helicopter might be superseded by more advanced forms of VTOL, Hafner said: 'The helicopter is a lifting device with a hover performance that is unlikely to be surpassed.'

FURTHER READING

Aerodynamics of the Helicopter, Alfred Gessow and Garry Myers, Fred Ungar, New York, 1967

Aircraft of the Royal Air Force since 1918, Owen Thetford, Putnam, London, 1971

Aviation. An Historical Survey from its Origins to the End of World War II, Charles H. Gibbs-Smith, HMSO, Science Museum, London, 1970

Bristol Aircraft since 1910, C. H. Barnes, Putnam, London, 1970

British Naval Aircraft since 1912, Owen Thetford, Putnam, London, 1971

Helicopter, The, J. Shapiro, Frederick Muller, London, 1957

Helicopter, The, H. F. Gregory, Allen and Unwin, London, 1949

Helicopters and Autogiros, Charles Gablehouse, Frederick Muller, London, 1968

Helicopters and Autogyros of the World, Paul Lambermont with Anthony Pirie, Cassell and Co Ltd, London, 1970

Helicopter and How it Flies, The, John Fay, Pitman and Co Ltd, London, 1967

Helicopters Work Like This, Basil Arkell and John W. R. Taylor, Phoenix House Ltd, London, 1965

Pocket Encyclopaedia of World Aircraft in Colour. Helicopters and other Rotorcraft, Since 1907, The, Kenneth Munson, Blandford Press, London, 1968

Story of the Winged S, The, Igor Sikorsky, Dodd Mead and Co, New York, 1967

Soviet Transport Aircraft since 1945, John Stroud, Putnam, London, 1968

United States Military Aircraft since 1909, Gordon Swanborough and Peter M. Bowers, Putnam, London, 1971

United States Navy Aircraft since 1911, Gordon Swanborough and Peter M. Bowers, Putnam, London, 1968

◀ BEA Helicopters' Sikorsky S-61N disembarking passengers at Scilly.

INDEX